PENGUIN
SELF-
STARTERS

Report Writing

Doris Wheatley has spent her life in Cambridge. Born in 1915, she was educated at the Perse Girls' School and Girton College, where she became Director of Studies in Archaeology and Anthropology. In 1966 she left the academic world to join a company, Cambridge Consultants (Training) Ltd. She became Managing Director in 1970 and eventually sole owner of the company, which she re-named Cambridge Communication as she decided this better described its activities. Her client list was once described as 'a roll-call of British industry'. She sold the company in 1984, although she continues to work as a freelance communication consultant.

Doris Wheatley was married and has twin children, a son and a daughter.

SERIES EDITORS: Stephen Coote and Bryan Loughrey

Report Writing

Doris Wheatley

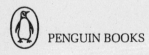

PENGUIN BOOKS

PENGUIN BOOKS

Published by the Penguin Group
27 Wrights Lane, London W8 5TZ, England
Viking Penguin Inc., 40 West 23rd Street, New York, New York 10010, USA
Penguin Books Australia Ltd, Ringwood, Victoria, Australia
Penguin Books Canada Ltd, 2801 John Street, Markham, Ontario, Canada L3R 1B4
Penguin Books (NZ) Ltd, 182–190 Wairau Road, Auckland 10, New Zealand

Penguin Books Ltd, Registered Offices: Harmondsworth, Middlesex, England

First published 1988

Filmset in Linotron Melior
Made and printed in Great Britain by
Hazell, Watson & Viney Limited
Member of BPCC plc
Aylesbury, Bucks

For my daughter and son,
Joanna Robson and Jacques Wheatley

Contents

Preface

Report writing is essentially an exercise in communication: transferring information from one person to another or from one group of people to another group. Reports are usually written by experts, and experts are notoriously bad at putting themselves in the position of non-experts. Reports are often aimed at non-experts, and this must always be remembered. The use of written language is important. Grammar, syntax and punctuation matter. Jargon has its place, but only if it can be understood.

Technical reports often must contain information – terms, quantities, formulae, equations – that is meaningless to the layperson, and yet the report will be read by many such. There are ways of dealing with this problem. Even to those who know, there must be uniformity, so universally accepted conventions must be used.

In my opinion, in the many publications I have read on report writing not enough emphasis has been placed on structure. A report of any sort, whether technical or not, must have a structure that displays its logic. Not only does this make it easy for the reader to take in what the report has to say, but also, in preparing it, the writer must marshal his thoughts, and this process enables him to get rid of the unnecessary material and repetitions that spoil so many arguments.

There is another element that is often involved – that of persuasion. There is one way of persuading, with which politicians are familiar, and that is deliberately to falsify the evidence. That method is crude and obvious; there are more subtle ways. Distortion can be achieved without falsification, by clever manipulation, by omission, by emphasis and by misusing graphs and diagrams. The only persuasion that this book is concerned with is that which comes from the presentation of facts in such a way that they reveal, not conceal, what the author of the report intends, and that is the accurate answer or answers to the question or questions that the report is designed to address.

There are many different kinds of report, but in all of them language, brevity, structure and relevance are the keynotes. Proposals that are 'selling' documents should be given careful attention. A curriculum vitae is one of these.

I was asked to write this book because for twenty years I ran a company concerned entirely with communication. Before that I taught social anthropology at the University of Cambridge. There was not as much difference between these two occupations, which made up my working life, as people like to make out. Now, in so-called retirement, I am still being consulted, and am still writing, about communication.

Acknowledgements

To acknowledge all the help I have been given in writing this book would take a lot of space! The following people deserve special mention.

I am grateful to Chief Superintendent J. D. Fuller of the Cambridgeshire Constabulary, and the Chief Fire Officer of the Cambridge Fire and Rescue Service, D. N. McCullum, for the valuable information they gave me.

Dr Paul Auton, Managing Director of Cambridge Consultants Ltd., who has enormous experience of highly technical reports, gave me some excellent advice.

Professor Davidson, one of the experts who conducted the Flixborough investigation, gave up his valuable time to tell me how that report came into being.

The Mistress of my college, Lady Warnock, was delightfully interesting in explaining how the report that bears her name was written.

I owe a very great debt to Dr Roy Hawkins of R. B. Hawkins Associates, who not only talked to me at length about the technical reports he writes as a forensic scientist but also introduced me to the Flixborough report, and for that I am particularly grateful.

Thanks are also owing to Terry Elcock, who, in the sixteen years we worked together when he ran my company's studio, taught me all I know about technical illustration.

To Muriel Lemon, who did far more than type my manuscript, and to Kay Harper, whose criticism was invaluable, I record my thanks.

For permission to reproduce copyright material, grateful acknowledgement is made to Jonathan Cape Ltd., and the estate of James Joyce for the extract from *A Portrait of the Artist as a Young Man*, and to HMSO Publications.

1 What Is a Report?

There seems to be no definitive answer to this question. The first pieces of paper called reports that most people come across are from their schools and are addressed to their parents or guardians. Implicit in producing these reports is the assumption that those who are responsible for children's education want to know how they are progressing in general and in each subject, how good they are at games, how they compare with other pupils of roughly the same age and what sort of people they are in the opinion of the school's staff.

These documents have printed headings and spaces for those who teach to fill in marks obtained and comments in the appropriate places. The structure of the reports is fixed, and only the marks and comments are different for each pupil.

The boy who, when this document is examined, is asked why he has such low marks in English, not to mention the comment 'barely literate', may well reply: 'I like science and I'm good at it. I hate English and I'm not so good at it, but I'm not as bad as Old Squeers makes out. He doesn't like me, so he always gives me the lowest possible marks for anything I produce.' The boy has a hunch that, although the comment has to bear some relation to the marks, which in their turn have to bear some relation to what he has produced in the examination, it is not completely objective. He suspects that if his mark were 79 per cent the comment would be something like, 'It is a mystery how he did so well in the examination as his term's work has been poor indeed.'

As a result of his poor report in English he may well be given special coaching. Also, as his science marks are good, and the comment is 'promising', he might start to think that he could become some sort of scientist one day.

So he thinks of a report as a structured piece of information, on paper, produced by those who have that information for those who want, or ought to want, to receive it. The information should be unbiased, but that is not always so. As a result of a report, action may be taken, and the report may suggest other possibilities. Our boy may have extra lessons in the first case, but a distant vision of becoming a scientist to cheer him up in the second.

Some people do not go to school. Imagine a boy who has a tutor and is taught at home. His father, who is in Australia, asks to be informed about his education progress. The tutor will write a letter to the father, giving much the same information as would be found on the document that a school sends out. Will this be a report? Does starting with 'Dear Sir Henry' and ending 'Yours sincerely' stop it from being a report, and will it be one if these are omitted? If, after the information about the boy's educational progress, the tutor adds on a few paragraphs about the flowers in the garden, the new vicar and the goings-on in the local, what will it be then? Again, if the tutor writes a letter about this and that and puts in a separate sheet describing the boy's achievements, is this a report with a covering letter?

Is it the form, or the content, or the purpose that is important in deciding whether or not what is written is a report? Let us look at dictionary definitions.

> To give an account of, esp. a formal, official, or requested account (*Chambers's Twentieth Century Dictionary*)
>
> An account prepared for the benefit of others, esp. one that provides information obtained through investigation (*Collins English Dictionary*)

It seems that the criteria for calling something a report are that it is:

formal

official

requested

for the benefit of others

and that the information has been obtained through investigation.

Let us take issue with 'requested'. The school report is not actually requested, but the assumption is that if it were not provided, it would certainly be asked for. Supposing an office manager is aware that equipment, say manual typewriters and an old-fashioned duplicator, is out of date, cumbersome and time-wasting, he might well write a report (or perhaps it would be a memorandum) to the managing director, asking for more up-to-date equipment. This report would not be 'requested', but it would be information that someone thought necessary to provide in order that appropriate action could be taken – almost the other way round.

In such a report there would certainly be no printed form to follow. The onus would be on the writer to collect his evidence, sort out what is relevant, put it in the right order, marshal his arguments and present a convincing case. Printed forms and set patterns can be, and often have to be, done without. But they serve a useful purpose where certain facts have to be discovered in all cases. The police force, the fire and rescue services, insurance companies and loss adjusters all use these forms for report writing. This ensures that nothing of importance is left out, and they cut down considerably the effort required to make the report. However, they can present problems. For example, boxes may have to be ticked:

Fire discovered by:	Persons	Sprinkler	Heat	Smoke	other (specify)

If a person saw the smoke, should boxes one and four be ticked? And if the smoke activated the sprinkler, boxes two and four?

People can be incredibly long-winded and not good at sifting what is relevant from what is not. This type of report form copes with this difficulty and saves time at both ends: in writing or producing the information, and in reading or assessing the information.

So far we have considered only what might be called 'simple' reports. A parent wants to know about his child's progress at school; the fire service wants information about a fire that it was called to; an insurance company wants to know when and how a car was damaged. There is also the other end of the scale: for example, if a jumbo jet crashes and all on board are killed. Aviation authorities, the airline, insurance companies, the manufacturers of the aircraft and of its engines and other components, and relatives of the dead all want to know what happened and why. A report on such an accident

cannot be produced by ticking boxes and writing a sentence here
and there.

On Saturday, 1 June 1974, just before five o'clock in the afternoon,
Nypro (UK) Limited's works at Flixborough in Northamptonshire
were virtually demolished by an explosion described as 'of warlike
dimensions'. As it was not an ordinary working day, and therefore
few employees were present, only twenty-eight people were killed
and thirty-six injured, and 1 821 houses and 167 business premises
were damaged to a greater or lesser degree. The Secretary of State for
Employment ordered an inquiry. He appointed people to hold an
investigation and to produce a report. That report, called *The Flixborough disaster: report of the Court of Inquiry*, was published by
HM Stationery Office in 1975. It is a superb example of report writing
and will be used throughout this book to exemplify how a report
should be written.

Interestingly enough, it begins 'To the Rt Hon. Michael Foot MP,
Secretary of State for Employment'. Is this different from 'Dear Sir
Henry'?

Are there different kinds of report? Is there anything fundamen-
tally different between the fire officer's report of the incident at 13
Duck Lane, when the chip pan caught fire with resultant damage to
the kitchen, and the Court of Inquiry's report on the Flixborough
disaster? The obvious difference is between the incidents. The one
was simple: the cause was obvious, the result was equally obvious
and so was the lesson to be learned from it. The other incident was
incredibly complex: neither the cause nor the result was obvious,
nor the lesson to be learned, until the cause was established.

In various books on report writing, classifications have been made
that assume that there are different kinds of report. One such class is
described as 'technical'. To a lot of people, 'technical' means something that only other people know about. Dictionary definitions of
the word are both more, and less, precise:

> of, relating to, or specializing in industrial, practical, or mechan-
> ical arts, rather than theoretical or abstract thinking *(Collins
> English Dictionary)*

> pertaining to art, esp. a useful art or applied science *(Chambers's
> Twentieth Century Dictionary)*

Would it be safe to accept that when we call a report 'technical' we are making the assumption that the writer possesses knowledge that belongs to a group of people familiar with a certain subject or discipline and that is not common knowledge? This subject or discipline might be, for example, engineering, medicine, physics, archaeology, pharmacology, architecture or computer science. If it is such a subject, and it probably is, then are we discussing a different kind of report, or a report that will have to deal with a special knowledge and its accompanying language or jargon?

No doubt an investigation into the advisability of relocation for a company could be written in language that everyone from the manual workers to the management could understand. It would need to contain a great deal of exact information, but information that would be expressed in what we would loosely call 'non-technical' terms. Would this be different in essence from a technical report such as that of the Flixborough disaster? It would most certainly be easier to write.

There is supposed to be a great division between literary people and scientists. Certainly each 'culture', as C. P. Snow called it, has its own snobbery. The scientists talk their jargon, which excludes the non-scientists, who in their turn show indifference to mere technology and turn their thoughts to higher things. This, of course, breaks down in practice, as the novelist uses his word processor and the scientist writes his theses, his papers and his reports, all of which need words.

Many people who write reports have also written a thesis, followed by papers. What is a 'thesis', and what is a 'paper', and are they different from a report? A thesis, or dissertation, is the writing-up of original research, usually for a doctorate. The research will probably have taken two or more years. The examiner is mainly concerned with the results of the research, but he is also concerned with method and with the general conduct and progress of the research. In general the thesis certainly is a report and, in an appropriate subject, a technical report. The examiner will be an expert in the subject and will easily understand what has been done and why, and will be able to evaluate the results. It has not been commissioned, and very few people are, alas, interested in the result. It may very well not be followed up. It is usually very long, as the researcher wants to make sure that he gets credit for everything he has done. As these people often end up writing reports proper, they then have to repeat this performance.

A 'paper' is also a kind of report. It is usually read aloud to an audience, whereas a thesis or a report is written, although it is often published later in a learned journal. It is intended primarily for the author's peers and not for people who do not share the same knowledge. Questions can be asked so that points that are not clear can be elucidated. The authors of 'papers', when they come to write reports, often forget that they are not writing for their peers.

Given that we have some idea of what reports (including technical reports) are, who writes them?

You and I do. If we have an insurance claim, the words 'Write a description of the accident and draw a diagram' appear on the claim form.

Police officers do. There are two types of police report: occurrence and offence. Report forms are provided, but police officers have to decide whether what they are reporting is an occurrence or an offence.

Fire officers do. They also have report forms to help them. Often after police officers or fire officers have made their reports, if anything seems unusual, a forensic scientist is called in, who also must make a report. This report can be very important indeed, as someone could be charged with arson or murder as a result of it, and in insurance claims millions of pounds can be at stake. The forensic scientist's report is usually too long and too detailed for forms to be used.

Loss adjusters do. The form of their reports is dictated by the insurance companies that employ them. Their reports are also important, as insurance claims depend on them. Sometimes, if the loss adjuster's report suggests the need, a forensic scientist is called in by the insurance company. There are Home Office forensic departments serving the police force, the C I D and the fire service, and there are independent companies, usually employed by insurance companies who could have to pay out millions of pounds in claims. The independent companies' reports must be understood by those employing them.

Certain employees of companies do. Those working in research and development have to make reports to management on their progress. Often what they are doing is technical, but they must make their results comprehensible to people not trained in that particular discipline.

There are companies specializing in research for other companies and for the armed forces. They must submit reports. One such report for the Ministry of Defence (unclassified or it would not be accessible) is in two volumes, one of 519 pages and the other 227: 746 pages of report!

At the other end of the scale from the form that you fill in when your car has an argument with another car is the outcome of a full-scale inquiry ordered by H M Government. The investigation will be done by a committee with one person presiding whose name the report will carry. In due course it will be published by H M Stationery Office, and its contents, therefore, become public property. Such a report is the Flixborough disaster report.

This model report has only fifty-one pages of text, which are supported by seventeen photographs and eleven diagrams.

> Formal Investigation into Accident on 1st June 1974 at the Nypro Factory at Flixborough
>
> Appointment of persons
> to hold investigation
>
> The Secretary of State, in exercise of his powers under Section 84 of the Factories Act 1961, hereby directs a formal investigation to be held under the said Section 84 into the accident which occurred on the 1st June 1974 at the factory of Nypro (UK) Limited at Flixborough.
>
> The Secretary of State, in further exercise of his said powers under the said Section 84, hereby appoints:
>
> ROGER JOCELYN PARKER, ESQ.
> Q C (Chairman)
> JOSEPH ALBERT POPE, ESQ.
> D Sc, Ph D, Wh Sch C Eng F I Mech E, (Deputy Chairman)
> JOHN FRANK DAVIDSON, ESQ.
> M A, Ph D, ScD, F R S, C Eng, F I Chem E, M I Mech E
> WILLIAM JAMES SIMPSON, ESQ.
> to hold the said investigation.
>
> The Secretary of State further appoints BERNARD MICHAEL O'REILLY, ESQ, F R I C, to be Secretary of the said investigation.

Michael Foot
Secretary of State for Employment

If there is any value in classifying reports, the only division that makes sense is between those that are made on an existing form and those that are not. The only sensible subdivision is between those that employ so-called 'technical terms' and those that don't (see Figure 1). One thing is common to all, and that is objectivity. This, as would be expected, is stressed when members of the police force and the fire service are trained to make their reports. Whether there is any difference between technical and non-technical reports, other than language, is open to doubt. Language, however, presents grave problems.

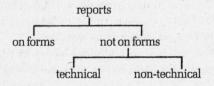

Figure 1

Just as the answer to 'Who writes reports?' is 'Almost everybody' and to 'Who writes technical reports?' is 'A great number of people', the answer to 'Who reads reports?' is also 'A great number of people'. Many reports are written for readers whose backgrounds and knowledge are different from those of the writer. The readership is a very important consideration when writing a report. The need to consider the readership will be discussed in detail in a later chapter.

Summary

A report presents information. This information is needed by some person or organization, and in many cases the information has been asked for. An investigation is made, which may be research or inquiry or both, and it must be objective. Then a report is presented. Some reports are made by filling in forms, and some are not.

The report must take into account its readership, which may or may not be knowledgeable in the field of the inquiry.

2 Is Objectivity Possible?

One definition of 'objectivity' is 'open to verification by an investigator'.

If two people, one a militant trade unionist, and the other a strong opponent of strike action, are watching a confrontation between the police and strikers, either in real life or on a film, it is unlikely that they will see the same things. Let us assume that they are both honest people wanting to discover the 'truth' about what is happening. It is very likely that one will see the aggression coming from the police, the other from the strikers. Both think they are being objective. It is easy to see what you expect to see, even with the best will in the world. If the two observers are not honest, they will certainly give different accounts of the aggression.

There is a different kind of situation, which could be called over-compensation. People who 'feel' an aversion to coloured people, knowing this is illogical and against all their principles, will go out of their way to favour or be particularly pleasant to anyone with dark skin. No doubt they also think they are being objective.

Different from these is the effect of 'set', defined in a dictionary of psychology as 'a condition of readiness for some special type of mental performance'. If you drop a pin on a carpet and search for it, any bright object – a sliver of foil for example – seems to jump out of the carpet towards you. If you are hoping for a telephone call, the sound of a bicycle bell makes you jump out of your seat. There is also the reverse phenomenon. You are looking for a book, the title of which you know, in a bookshelf. You think the book has a green cover, and you pass over it many times because, in fact, it has a blue cover, so, in spite of its title being clearly visible, you don't see it.

In 1901 Freud published *Psychopathology of Everyday Life* and drew attention to the fact that our conscious minds are sometimes under the control of our unconscious minds. We forget things, we make mistakes, we see things wrongly, we hear things wrongly, we have accidents. These errors all have a meaning and a purpose, Freud said. They are particularly difficult to guard against, as they are unconscious. (One of the most penetrating remarks made about Freudian psychology is 'The most difficult thing about the unconscious is that it is unconscious.')

Then there is that distressing thing, 'the evidence of our senses'. We can all see for ourselves that the sun goes round the earth, yet we believe, and few of us have questioned it, that the earth goes round the sun. In other words, we don't always believe the evidence of our senses.

Objectivity is, we are often told, the essence of the scientific attitude. Scientists assess facts and test hypotheses without attention to what they expect or would like the results to be. In view of the hindrances to complete objectivity we can only assume that most scientists, most of the time, do their best to achieve what is clearly impossible.

There are two other causes of lack of objectivity: self-deception and deliberate fraud. Deliberate fraud can also be subdivided into that which is intended to lead people up the garden path, and that which is the result of a burning conviction that lacks evidence to support it (see Figure 2).

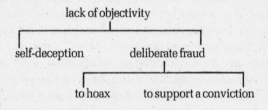

Figure 2

We will examine an instance of each of these three types.

An American physician and scientist, S. G. Morton, who lived in Philadelphia and died in 1851, made a collection of over 1 000 human skulls. He started with the hypothesis that the volume of the skull is a measure of intelligence. Certainly the volume of the skull of *Homo sapiens* is larger than that of the various forms of early man. What intelligence is is very difficult to say. The most reliable definition is 'the ability to do well in intelligence tests'. Therefore, the hypothesis was of doubtful validity. However, Morton measured the volumes of all his skulls, and these measurements were published. From his statistical evidence he produced a grading:

1   Whites   Western Europeans
                             Jews
2   American Indians
3   Blacks

which was exactly what he wanted and expected to find. Morton was a highly respected scientist. The amazing feature of the story is that he published all his statistical evidence, and it was reprinted many times. His scientific colleagues did not question his conclusions. It was more than a century later that Stephen Jay Gould, a Harvard palaeontologist, re-examined the evidence. He used Morton's own figures and found that all races have approximately the same skull volume. In fact, skull size is related to total body size. The astonishing thing about this story is the fact that Morton hoodwinked not only himself but also all his colleagues, who could have examined his figures as Gould did a century later. Had he wished to cheat, he would, presumably, have fudged his figures.

For archaeologists and palaeontologists one of the most remarkable whodunnits is the story of Piltdown man or *Eoanthropus*. Apparently, side by side in a tertiary geological deposit were found parts of a thick but human-looking cranium and a very ape-like jaw. The discoverer, Charles Dawson, a well-known amateur archaeologist, consulted Arthur Smith Woodward of the British Museum about his discoveries. This new 'evidence' upset all ideas about the evolution of man, particularly when in Africa skulls were found that were exactly opposite to Piltdown, with human-like jaws and ape-like craniums.

In the 1950s modern methods of dating archaeological and palaeontological finds were developed, and it was soon revealed that the Piltdown skull was a forgery. Whether Dawson was the forger has not been established. Some think that he had neither the skill nor the access to the fossils used to make up the odd man out in the evolutionary process. Whoever was the forger, he certainly had his money's worth, as a doubt was cast on the course of evolution, which lasted for forty years. It is easy to be wise after the event, but although doubts were expressed when Piltdown man was 'found', no one really challenged Dawson, who died, greatly revered, in 1916. It is worth noting that after his death nothing more was found in the gravel pit.

This raises an important query: if one discovery or observation or result in an experiment is out of line with all the rest, how should it be treated? It would obviously be wrong to ignore it, as it might be of vital significance, however inconvenient it is. It is tempting to discard a piece of evidence that will upset a theory, but this must not be done. It must be rigorously examined, and discarded only if it is proven to be of no importance.

Sir Cyril Burt's research on identical twins had an important place in the debate about the inheritability of intelligence. He received his knighthood for his contribution to educational psychology and was described as 'Britain's most eminent educational psychologist' when he died in 1971. Burt's theories of the inheritability and immutability of intelligence had great influence on the whole structure of the educational system in England. He also achieved renown in the U S A, but it was there that his reputation was destroyed. Leon Kamin, from Princeton, examined Burt's statistics and found them wholly unacceptable. In 1976 *The Times* printed an article, written by its medical correspondent, accusing Burt of fraud. This created a furore, but when his biographer, Leslie Hearnshaw, examined Burt's diaries and letters, he was forced to the conclusion that Burt had faked at least some of the evidence to support his theories. Even his assistants appeared to be mostly fictitious. Yet Burt had hoodwinked psychologists on both sides of the Atlantic for thirty years and was enormously powerful.

These three cases show different aspects of lack of objectivity. Morton certainly collected and measured his skulls, but to confirm his racist beliefs he drew the wrong conclusions from his published figures. Dawson and/or another perpetrated a deliberate hoax and achieved fame through it. Burt, who was convinced that his theories of intelligence were true, invented the data to support them. The work of all three was accepted by their scientific colleagues.

It is possible to draw different conclusions from an objective examination of the data gathered. An example of this can be seen in the Flixborough disaster report.

The immediate cause of the explosion was the 'ignition and rapid acceleration of deflagration, possibly to the point of detonation, of a massive vapour cloud formed by the escape of cyclohexane under at least a pressure of 8.8kg/cm^2 and a temperature of 155°C'. This escape came from a section of the plant known as Section 25A, 'devoted to the production of cyclohexanone and cyclohexanol by the oxidation of cyclohexane with air in the presence of a catalyst'.

What does this mean to the layperson? Should a basic course in chemistry be added to the report? Anyone likely to read this report will know, however vaguely, that a reactor is 'a container where a chemical reaction takes place'. However, 'deflagration' may defeat some people. It is the noun from deflagrate: 'to burn suddenly, generally with flame and crackling noise'. But there is little or no difficulty in following what happened. Without knowing the chemistry, the ordinary reader can work out:

1 that the explosion was due to an escape of gas under pressure and at a high temperature;
2 that the escape was in the section called 25A where a certain process took place.

This seems all that is necessary to go on with the argument. In Section 25A there had been six reactors, and one of them had developed a crack, so it was removed, and a by-pass assembly was installed. It was determined that the explosion was caused by the rupture of this by-pass assembly.

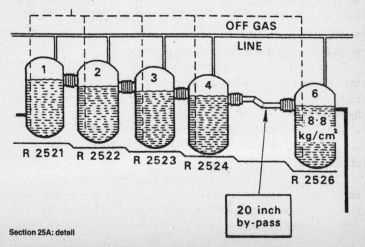

Section 25A: detail

Three possible reasons were discovered for the rupture.

1 The 20-inch hypothesis: rupture of the by-pass through internal pressure;
2 The two-stage hypothesis: rupture of the assembly in two stages – a small tear in the bellows from excess pressure leading to an escape and minor explosion, causing the final rupture;
3 The 8-inch hypothesis: rupture of the 8-inch pipe (in which a 50-inch split was discovered after the explosion) leading to a minor explosion, causing the rupture of the assembly.

The two-stage hypothesis was soon discarded after experimental investigation, which left the 20-inch and 8-inch hypotheses, each of which had its protagonists.

As well as the evidence from the wreckage, eye-witness, film and photographic evidence was considered.

> Clear evidence from the wreckage and other sources could not be over-ridden but if other evidence left the relative probabilities of the alternative hypotheses evenly balanced then eye-witness evidence and photographic evidence could tip the scale one way or other.

The sound sequence that would have occurred if the 8-inch hypothesis had been correct is beautifully described in the report as:

> Bang ⸺ escape and rumble ⸺ bigger bang ⸺ bigger escape and rumble ⸺ final bang

In fact, it emerged that the sequence was:

> noise ⸺ rumble ⸺ bang

which supported the 20-inch hypothesis.

The 8-inch hypothesis was examined in very great detail. After discussion of one point, this comment was made:

> We have dealt with this particular point in some detail for it appears to us to be a good example of the way in which the enthusiasm for the 8-inch hypothesis felt by its proponents has led them to overlook obvious defects which in other circumstances they would not have failed to realize.

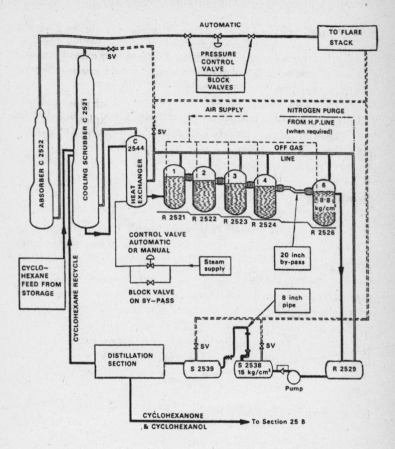

AUTOMATIC

PRESSURE
CONTROL
VALVE

BLOCK
VALVES

TO FLARE
STACK

SV

AIR SUPPLY

NITROGEN PURGE

FROM H.P. LINE
(when required)

OFF GAS
LINE

SV

C
2544

HEAT EXCHANGER

ABSORBER C 2522

COOLING SCRUBBER C 2521

1 2 3 4 6
8·8 kg/cm³

R 2521 R 2522 R 2523 R 2524 R 2526

CONTROL VALVE
AUTOMATIC
OR MANUAL

CYCLOHEXANE RECYCLE

CYCLO-
HEXANE
FEED FROM
STORAGE

Steam
supply

20 inch
by-pass

BLOCK VALVE
ON BY-PASS

8 inch
pipe

DISTILLATION
SECTION

SV   SV

S 2539   S 2538
          15 kg/cm³

R 2529

Pump

CYCLOHEXANONE
& CYCLOHEXANOL

To Section 25 B

CYCLOHEXANE OXIDATION
PLANT SECTION 25 A
Simplified flow diagram (not to scale)

Cyclohexane loop	———	SV =	Safety valve
Off gas	———	R =	Reactor
Safety valve vent	=====	S =	Separator
Nitrogen (when required)	—·—·—	C =	Column
Air (not operating at time of disaster).	- - - - -		

A very apt comment on objectivity. The way of dealing with the situation is also well stated by the Court of Inquiry:

> We have considered the 8-inch hypothesis at what may perhaps appear unnecessary length. We have done so because its proponents were all highly qualified in their respective fields and because the hypothesis was given considerable attention in some sections of the press before it had been fully examined.

However difficult it is to achieve objectivity, it is an essential part of good report writing and must be striven for. A knowledge of one's own prejudices, fads and foibles is a good starting-point.

Summary

Complete objectivity is very difficult, if not impossible, to achieve. Strongly held beliefs will cause people to see or hear some things rather than others. Such beliefs can also make them overcompensate for what they consider to be their own lack of objectivity. Similarly, people see and hear what they want to see and hear. The tricks played by the unconscious mind also affect objectivity.

There are two other causes of lack of objectivity: self-deception and deliberate fraud. Self-deception may cause results to be interpreted wrongly. Deliberate fraud may arise from a desire to hoax or a desire to provide evidence that has not been obtained to back up beliefs.

If, in an inquiry, interpretation of evidence is thought to arise from strong convictions, then that evidence must be very carefully examined before the interpretation can be rejected or accepted.

3 Words

At last it seems that some people are beginning to demand that what they read and hear in their own language should be intelligible to them. Societies set up to propagate the gospel of plain English give prizes for finding the worst (or best?) examples of meaningless English. The writers of pension booklets usually provide some excellent entries for these competitions, as do those who write the instructions for filling in forms, many of which have defeated perfectly intelligent people, and those who produce user manuals for equipment in the house, which are, more often than not, useless. What is 'plain English'?

There is no simple answer to that question. Probably the best-known attempt to produce 'plain English' is that put forward by C. K. Ogden in 1929, which he called Basic English. This was not so much to make English easy to understand as to provide a universal language, 'debabelizing' as he called it. The vocabulary was cut down to 850 words, which he claimed could do the work of 20,000. The 850 words consist of 600 nouns, 150 adjectives and 100 'operations', which include verbs. For example, 'prepare' becomes 'get ready', and it is claimed that such combinations of words can replace 4 000 ordinary verbs. Basic English is 'idiomatic English with no literary pretensions but clear and precise at the level for which it was designed'.

Not so well known, except among those who are particularly concerned with communication, is the Fog Index. An American, Robert Gunning, in his book *The Technique of Clear Writing*, published in New York in 1952, describes writing that is difficult to read as 'foggy'. From this came his 'Fog Index' (F I) by which it is possible, he claims, to measure the readability of what has been written. To make for easy reading, long words and long sentences should be avoided.

To find the Fog Index:

1 Choose several samples of 100 words each.
2 Divide the number of words by the number of sentences. This gives the average number of words in each sentence.
3 Count the number of words that have three or more syllables in each sample of 100 words. Ignore:
   (a) words that have capital letters
   (b) combination words like 'lawnmower' or 'handwritten'
   (c) words ending in -ed or -es, like 'frustrated' or 'redresses'.

This gives the number of 'difficult' words in the passage.

4 To calculate the F I, add together the answers to 2 and 3, and multiply the answer by 0.4.

The F I is graded:

less than 10	easy to read
11–12	top 20 per cent of twelve-year-olds
13	top 20 per cent of sixteen-year-olds
14–16	first-year university students
17	university graduates

Let us examine this passage from an unclassified report written for the Ministry of Defence.

> In logic systems design the choice of, and indeed for, codes depends on the size of the system, its function, the word length of the data, the complexity of the decoder for a particular code, the statistics of the noise, failure characteristics of the technology etc. A particular area of digital systems that has benefited greatly from the use of codes is that of memories. Parity bits are quite common in small-sized R O M S and Hamming S E C/D E D codes in larger memories. The latter are especially useful in fault-tolerant memory designs based on bit slice architecture where each bit of the/memory word is contained in physically separate chips.

The 100 words end at the oblique line. There are eighty words in

three sentences, so the average number of words per sentence is
26.66. There are sixteen words of three or more syllables. Therefore
the F I is:

$$26.66 + 16 = 42.66 \times 0.4 = 17.06$$

According to the grading, this can be read easily only by a university
graduate. These are the words with three or more syllables:

complexity	decoder
particular (twice)	digital
statistics	
characteristics	
technology	
benefited	
memories (twice)	
especially	
tolerant	
architecture	
memory	
parity (bits)	

The words in the first column are understood by most adults,
whether university-educated or not, although 'architecture' is used
in a special way. 'Parity' presents difficulties as it qualifies 'bits'. Not
caught in the F I net, oddly enough, is 'bit-sliced', which is not an
everyday phrase.

It is open to doubt whether the words of three or more syllables in
this passage make reading more difficult than words such as 'bit-
sliced'. In fact, what makes it almost impossible for the layperson to
understand has nothing to do with long words or long sentences.
The difficulty arises because the words that are used have what we
might call an 'ordinary' meaning, but they also have another meaning in a particular technology. As the report was not written for lay
people it does not matter, but it does indicate that the F I is of
questionable value in technical writing. It is doubtful whether a
graduate in any arts subject would be happy with the language of
this report. (It is worth noting, by contrast, that all the popular
magazines and newspapers with a very high circulation have an F I
of ten or under.)

The enemies of plain English, we are told, are technical terminology, or jargon, and gobbledegook. As sciences develop, new words come into existence. In this age of the motor car the words 'gear', 'carburettor', 'battery', 'clutch', 'bonnet', 'boot', 'antifreeze', 'puncture' and 'windscreen' are in most people's vocabularies. At the beginning of this century bonnets and boots were things to wear, and few but engineers would know the meaning of the other words. Even bicycles had solid tyres, so 'puncture' would only mean a hole. There is a derogatory overtone in 'jargon', and to most people it refers to language used by an élite to which they do not belong. There is a clever advertisement for a video recorder:

> Audio frequency response, ($\pm$6dB), 20 hz–20khz.
> Dynamic range, more than 80dB.
> Total harmonic distortion, less than 0.8%.
> Wow and flutter, less than 0.008%.
> Channel separation more than 55dB.
> Signal to noise ratio, 65dB.

> or

> You ain't seen, or heard, nothing yet.

Only hi-fi enthusiasts will understand the specifications, but the misquotation from President Reagan will make the message clear to those reading the advertisement.

Whether technical terminology should be used in a report depends on three factors. The most important one is the readers for whom the report is being written. Another is whether there will eventually be a wider readership. The last is whether the report can be written without using it.

If a report is written for people completely familiar with the technical language, it would be silly to avoid using it. Generally, technical terms are a short way of saying something that would take a great number of ordinary words to describe. If it is written for non experts then great care must be taken to use non-technical language wherever this is possible. Before it is finalized it must always be tried out on either one of those for whom the report is being written or someone with a similar lack of knowledge. If technical terms must be used, they must be clearly defined. This can be done in the text or in a footnote the first time the term is used, or a glossary can be prepared and put at the beginning, not the end, of the report. There is something to be said for each of these three ways. If the definition is in the text, the reader does not have to break off while reading, look to the bottom of the page and then find the place again. If most readers will know the terms, footnotes may be most suitable, as only those unfamiliar with the terms will need to consult the notes. If there is a glossary and terms come more than once, readers will know exactly where to find the definitions.

Governmental reports will be read by members of both Houses of Parliament with different degrees of knowledge of the subjects and, if they are of wide interest, by many of the public as well. The *Report of the Committee of Inquiry into Human Fertilization and Embryology* is such a report and has the additional difficulty of being on highly controversial subjects involving ethical and moral issues. Members of the Committee of Inquiry were not by any means all doctors, gynaecologists or embryologists. The chairwoman, Lady Warnock, is a philosopher. Perhaps the composition of the committee is one of the reasons why the report is completely comprehensible to ordinary readers, as the members themselves had first to understand the issues involved.

Embryology is a subject that can be written about without a great deal of technical language. Those terms that have been used in the report are defined in footnotes:

> This report distinguishes between *in vitro* meaning 'in a glass',
> and *in vivo* meaning 'in the body'.
> A 'dominant' condition is one in which the disorder will manifest
> itself in all individuals who possess the gene responsible for the
> condition.

Perhaps the committee avoided technical terms too strenuously in referring to 'eggs' for human ova, and 'egg collection' for obtaining ova. There is in these terms an obtrusive suggestion of the farmyard or of birds nesting that 'ova collection' would avoid.

'Jargon' has become a derogatory term because people use technical language in two unfortunate ways. One way is to establish the one-upmanship of 'I know a lot of things you don't know.' The completely erroneous corollary to this is, 'If I know something you don't know, then I am more intelligent than you.' This is particularly common in the area of high technology. The other way is the unthinking one: 'If I know this you must too.' 'Any fool knows that you can't change gear in a manual car without using the clutch' has jeopardized a number of relationships.

There follows an extract from a report on who may marry whom in an East African society:

> No Gisu may marry a member of his own, his mother's or paternal grandmother's lineage. Two people who can trace descent from a common ancestor or ancestress three generations removed from themselves, through any genealogical connection, may not marry. The children of men circumcised at the same homestead may not marry, nor may the children of blood-brothers. These prohibitions emphasize the ties of kinship and underline the primary importance of the minimal lineage. Outside this group agnates may become affines. Marriage prohibitions mark out those people with whom ties are a matter of descent and filiation: these ties are acquired at birth and cannot normally be broken. Affinal ties, by contrast, are a matter of choice and result from a contract which can be rescinded.

It would be very difficult for a non-anthropologist reader to work this out, although the subjects, marriage and relationships, are common to all human society.

The word 'jargon', according to the revised edition of Fowler's *Modern English Usage*, is 'perhaps the most variously applied of a large number of words that are in different senses interchangeable'. For 'gobbledegook' one finds 'see jargon', but 'gobbledegook' is not one of the interchangeable words listed. Fowler says that 'jargon' should be used for 'the sectional vocabulary of a science, art, class, sect, trade or profession, full of technical terms'. So what is gobbledegook? It is better to distinguish it from jargon and confine its use to 'pretentious language e.g. as characterized by obscure phraseology' (*Collins English Dictionary*) Another of its characteristics, in the author's opinion, is long, convoluted sentences.

It is not likely that gobbledegook like this:

> The union of growing productivity and growing destruction; the brinkmanship of annihilation; the surrender of thought, hope,

> and fear to the decisions of the powers that be; the preservation of
> misery in the face of unprecedented wealth constitute the most
> impartial indictment – even if they are not the *raison d'être* of this
> society but only its by-product: its sweeping rationality, which
> propels efficiency and growth, is itself irrational.

would find its way into a report. But it is conceivable that, in a report
to the Board, on a new scheme, a pensions manager might write:

> 'Final pensionable wage' is the average of the member's pension-
> able wage on the three 6th days of April preceding the normal
> retirement date, or the date of retirement or death whichever is
> the earlier.

Fortunately there is a revolt against gobbledegook, and it has become
fashionable to expose outstanding examples in newspapers and on
television shows. There are awards for the worst examples. Below is
one winner, perpetrated by the Inland Revenue.

> Take notice that by virtue of Regulation 27A of the Income Tax
> (Employments) Regulations 1973 (as inserted by Regulation 3 in
> the Income Tax (Employments) (No. 15) Regulations 1985) Regu-
> lation 8A of the Income Tax . . . you are required to pay either the
> amount specified (A above) or an amount which you declared to
> be the full amount which you are liable to pay for the period (B
> below).

In the television series *Yes, Minister* and *Yes, Prime Minister* Sir
Humphrey Appleby, a civil servant, often speaks in gobbledegook.

> The relationship, which I might tentatively venture to aver has
> been not without some degree of reciprocal utility and perhaps
> even occasional gratification, is approaching the point of irrever-
> sible bifurcation, and to be brief is in the propinquity of its
> ultimate regrettable termination.

He explains.

> In other words, I am on my way out.

It is doubtful whether writers of gobbledegook ever speak it as Sir
Humphrey does, but he sets out deliberately to befuddle,

As well as unnecessary jargon and gobbledegook, to be avoided are vogue-words and phrases. These usually, by their nature, have a short life, but they are irritating. 'Basically', when it doesn't mean basically, is a current one. 'In this day and age' and 'at this moment in time' have had too long a life already, as has 'at the end of the day'. Clichés are also best avoided. Scientists and technologists should not 'explore avenues' or 'turn over stones'.

Are we to assume that those who write technical reports must use short words, write short sentences, avoid jargon and, above all else, avoid gobbledegook? Too many short words and short sentences might sound like a child's reading-book. As has been said already, a lot depends on who will read the report. There is never any particular virtue in using long words and long sentences, but neither is there any virtue in self-consciously avoiding them. There can be little point in gobbledegook, and all power to the elbows of those who are de-bunking it. Jargon is permissible if those for whom the report is intended are familiar with it.

A golden rule is never to write anything you couldn't say easily.

Summary

There is no simple answer to the question 'What is plain English?' Basic English has only 850 words, which its originator claims can do the work of 20 000. Application of the Fog Index shows whether a writer has used too many long words and long sentences for easy comprehension. Jargon and gobbledegook are the chief enemies of plain English. Jargon is an in-language and presents problems only to those who do not understand it. Gobbledegook consists of tortuous constructions more than of obscure language. There seems to be no place for gobbledegook. The most important consideration for report writers is to keep in mind *all the time* the people who will read their reports. To read out loud what they have written can be a good corrective.

4 Illustrations

Words are probably the most important tools of communication, but however excellent a description may be, it is sometimes very difficult, even impossible, for the reader to visualize what has been described. Illustrations can often greatly extend a reader's understanding of a report.

The word 'illustration' suggests to most people something extra to a piece of writing. In technical publications, and other types of report, illustrations are an important part of conveying information. Illustrations in non-technical writing always provide information, but they are usually the artist's idea of what something looked like. A technical publication also may contain an illustration of something that is only imagined, but it will be the author's idea, which is then communicated to an artist, who will have to satisfy the author by representing the idea accurately.

A **photograph**, or perhaps a series of photographs, is an obvious way of indicating what something looks like – front, back and side views, top and bottom. Colours can be shown with reasonable accuracy.

A camera is not always to hand when something unexpected happens, such as an accident, the start of a fire or an explosion, but when there is one it can provide invaluable evidence. An amateur 8 mm film was taken at Flixborough only a minute or two after the explosion. The Court of Inquiry 'viewed it more than once, both in its original 8 mm form and in a 16 mm version prepared by the B B C, and we inspected it frame by frame in a viewer also on a number of occasions'.

A **film** can be extremely useful because a sequence of events can be seen that individual photographs could not show accurately, as a certain interval must occur between one shot and the next.

Polaroid cameras are a great help to technical illustrators. If a small machine or piece of apparatus has to be drawn, it can be taken into the studio. This is not possible if the object is fixed, or very large, or very heavy. The advantage of a Polaroid camera is that the photographs can be seen a few minutes after they have been taken, and if they are not satisfactory, they can be taken again. In this way more than one visit to the place where the object is situated is unnecessary.

Photographs, however, have their drawbacks. Shadows can blur details, and a clear **line drawing** can be more satisfactory. A photograph would need to be very large to show clearly all the details that can be shown in a small line drawing. Photographs are also more difficult to reproduce in a technical report than drawings, so it is better to use photographs only when they add considerably to the text and other illustrations.

Another kind of illustration is the **diagram**. The *Collins English Dictionary* defines this as 'a sketch, outline or plan demonstrating the form or working of something'. Those familiar with 'whodunnits' will have seen the kind of diagram or plan that shows the relationship between the library where the murder was committed and the other rooms, passages and doors (not to mention the shrubbery). This makes it easier for the reader to work out exactly what happened. A proper plan is 'a drawing to scale of a horizontal section through a building taken at a given level'. From the plan in Figure 3 it can be seen that the ground floor of the house has a front door, an entrance hall, a staircase, two rooms and a kitchen, each with one window, and a back door leading into the kitchen. Apart from their size, we cannot tell what the rooms look like. The diagram from the Flixborough report, represented on page 19 of this book, is invaluable for appreciating how the disaster happened, but it would be impossible accurately to visualize the reactors and the ruptured 20-inch by-pass without the photographs.

We must conclude that the functions of photographs and diagrams are different, and sometimes a combination of both is necessary if the aim of illustrations – to inform – is to be fully accomplished.

A simple arrangement of words with arrows or lines to show connections can often be more effective than words alone. The structure of a company, for example, could be shown as in Figure 4. Similarly the process of producing a form could be shown as in Figure 5.

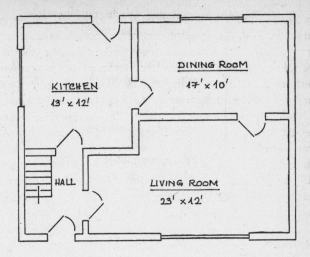

Figure 3

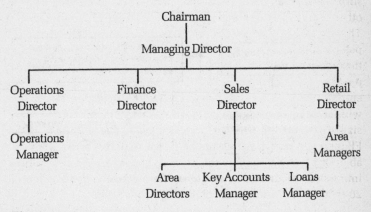

Figure 4

One form of diagram is the **flow-chart algorithm**. An algorithm is a means of solving a problem by considering only those factors that are relevant to that problem. In Figures 6 and 8 are two versions of an algorithm for eliminating hum in audio equipment.

Unfortunately algorithms are very difficult to write, and it is even more difficult to produce an elegant layout. In the second version

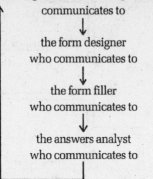

The person/organization needing the information
communicates to

the form designer
who communicates to

the form filler
who communicates to

the answers analyst
who communicates to

Figure 5

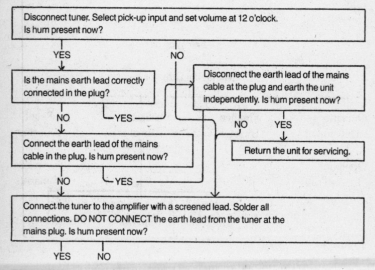

TO ELIMINATE HUM

Disconnect tuner. Select pick-up input and set volume at 12 o'clock. Is hum present now?

YES — Is the mains earth lead correctly connected in the plug?

NO — Disconnect the earth lead of the mains cable at the plug and earth the unit independently. Is hum present now?

NO — Connect the earth lead of the mains cable in the plug. Is hum present now?

YES — Return the unit for servicing.

Connect the tuner to the amplifier with a screened lead. Solder all connections. DO NOT CONNECT the earth lead from the tuner at the mains plug. Is hum present now?

YES   NO

Figure 6

(Figure 8) the boxes have been positioned so that there are no crossed lines, and the algorithm moves from top to bottom and from left to right. Also the questions have been removed from the instructions and put in separate boxes of a different shape (see Figure 7).

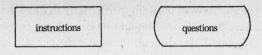

Figure 7

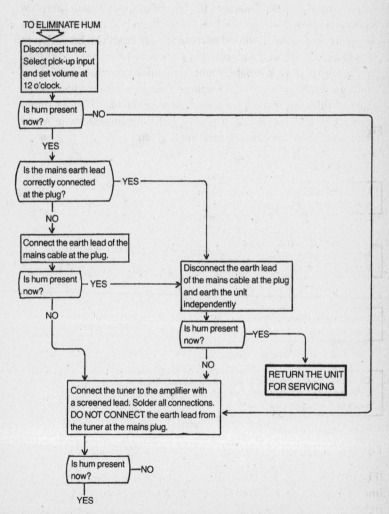

Figure 8

A very popular form of diagram, particularly in financial reports, is the **pie chart**. This shows proportions clearly unless some of the slices are very small. It is difficult to see at a glance the relationship between £17,178,450 and £137,427,450, but it is easy to see from a pie chart that the smaller number is approximately one-eighth of the larger (see Figure 9). If some of the 'slices' are very small, there are various ways of dealing with this. One of them is to use the magnifying-glass technique. Detailed parts of the pie chart can be drawn to an enlarged scale, as if a magnifying glass were being used, as shown in Figure 10. If appropriate, some companies substitute pictures of their products for 'pies' – for example, beer in mugs for a brewery or cans of different sizes for a container manufacturer. These pictograms can add interest to a report, but the proportions must be accurate, otherwise false information is given.

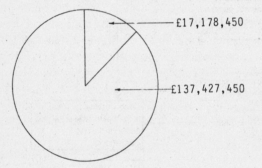

Figure 9

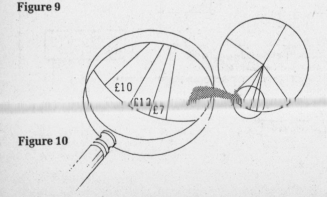

Figure 10

Bar charts are also effective. Strictly speaking a bar chart should use a single ruled line, but blocks are usually used (see Figure 11).

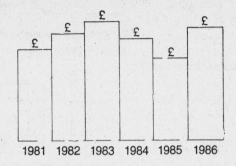

Figure 11

Not all diagrams are as clear and helpful as they might be. It is usually easy to compare one straight line with another, but some shapes make comparison difficult. The larger figure in each of the pairs in Figure 12 is four times the size of the smaller figure. There are well-known devices for making lines and objects of the same size look different. The best known are probably the Müller-Lyer illusions (see Figure 13). The diagrams demonstrate that illustrations do not always provide useful information. Unless carefully selected, they can be misleading and can confuse rather than clarify a reader's understanding.

Figure 12

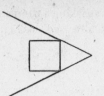

Is this a square or a rectangle?

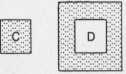

Which section is longer, A or B?

Are these rectangles
the same length or different?

Is square C smaller than square D?

Figure 13

Very different from diagrams and photographs are technical illustrations. Technical illustrators are very skilled and highly trained,
and few authors should attempt to do their work.

Orthographic drawings are made up of plans of the back, front
and side elevations and the top view of an object, all drawn to scale
(see Figure 14). They contain essential information for a designer or
a manufacturer but they are not particularly useful for those who
want to see what an object looks like. The finished article is shown in
Figure 15.

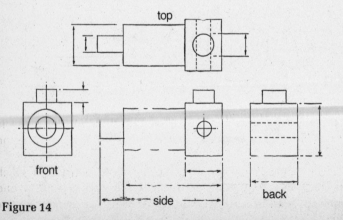

Figure 14

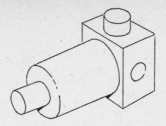

Figure 15

In contrast to orthographic drawings are **isometric drawings**, in which length, breadth and thickness are shown in a single view. No attention is paid to perspective, so all lines that are parallel in the object are shown as parallel in the drawing. A true isometric drawing has an angle of 120° between the planes. Isometric drawings can be produced by authors who have no skill in drawing, as the only equipment that is needed is a 60° set square, but they look peculiar because of lack of perspective (see Figure 16).

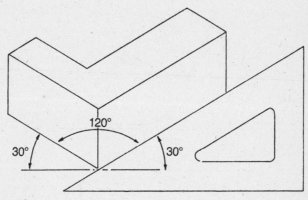

Figure 16

A **perspective drawing** (see Figure 17) shows an object as it is seen. Parallel lines appear to be able to meet at some point in the distance.

The illustrator must beware of ambiguous perspective, of which the two best-known examples are the Necker cube (Figure 18) and the Schröder staircase (Figure 19), both of which can be seen in more

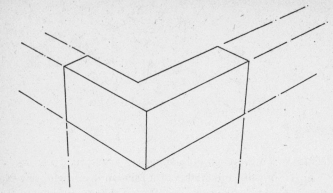

Figure 17

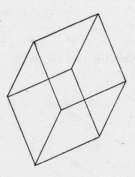

Figure 18

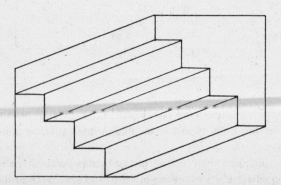

Figure 19

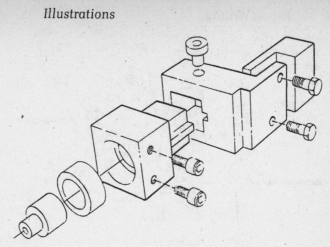

Figure 20

than one way. Blinking usually makes them change. Line drawings can be used to show things that photographs cannot show.

It is not always possible to take something apart to see how it has been put together, but an **exploded view diagram** makes this clear (see Figure 20). Equally, it is often difficult to look inside a machine to see how it works. A **cut-away illustration** can show this (see Figure 21).

A drawing can be used to show the location of a part, and an enlargement of the part makes it possible to see it in detail (see Figure 22).

A sequence of illustrations showing how a process or operation is carried out cuts to a minimum the explanatory text that is needed (see Figures 23 to 26). Drawings such as these can be produced only by a professional technical illustrator and should not be attempted by the writer.

Graphs are used to show the relationship between two variable quantities. For example, the graphs in Figure 27 (see p. 42) investigate whether an increase in advertising costs corresponds to an increase in quantities sold. If a line is drawn to join the points plotted on the graph, then the straighter it is, the closer the relationship between the two variables. The first graph indicates no relationship; the second indicates some (as more money is spent, more sales are made). A perfect relationship would produce a straight line.

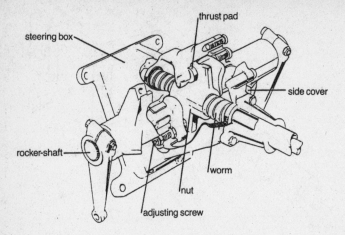

Figure 21

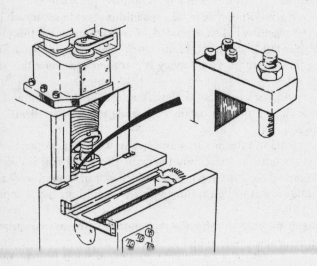

Figure 22

opposite **Figures 23–26**

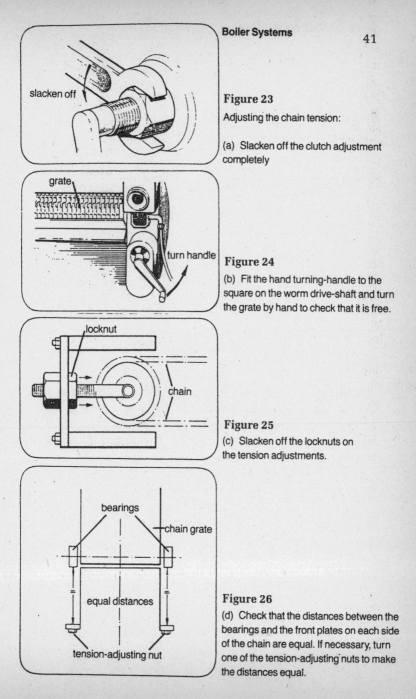

Figure 23

Adjusting the chain tension:

(a) Slacken off the clutch adjustment completely

Figure 24

(b) Fit the hand turning-handle to the square on the worm drive-shaft and turn the grate by hand to check that it is free.

Figure 25

(c) Slacken off the locknuts on the tension adjustments.

Figure 26

(d) Check that the distances between the bearings and the front plates on each side of the chain are equal. If necessary, turn one of the tension-adjusting nuts to make the distances equal.

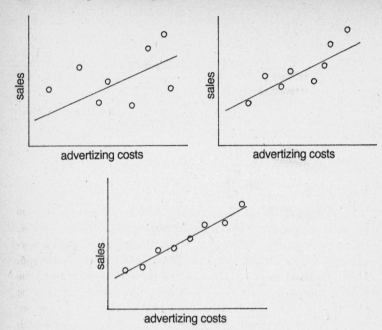

Figure 27

Reading tables of figures is tedious, and it is difficult to make comparisons unless the differences or similarities between figures are extremely obvious. The use of graphs, such as those shown in Figure 28, means that the presentation of quantitative information is much clearer and is simpler for the reader to understand.

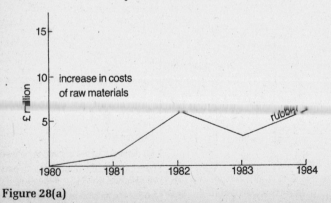

Figure 28(a)

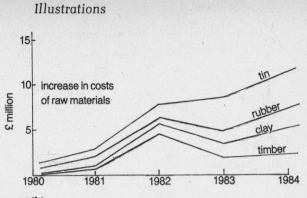

Figure 28(b)

Break-even charts enable one to read off how many goods must be sold at what price to recoup the sum that they cost. For example, Figure 29 shows that if items are bought at £20 for the first twenty-five and £4 for each additional twenty-five, 125 items will cost £36. This is the **cost line** on which the cost of any quantity of items can be seen. If the price is set at 25p per item, the **income line** can be plotted: the seller will get £12.50 for fifty, £25 for 100 and so on. Where the cost line and the income line cross is the point at which the cost of producing the items is covered; this is the break-even point. If the items are sold at 25p each, the break-even point will be 175 items (see Figure 30); and more than this must be sold to make a profit. (It must be remembered that this calculation does not allow for the added cost of selling the items.) If they are sold at 40p per item, the break-even point will be 60 (see Figure 31). The obvious difficulty is in estimating how many items are likely to be sold.

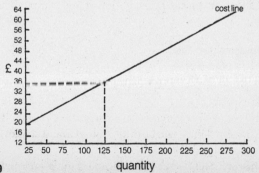

Figure 29

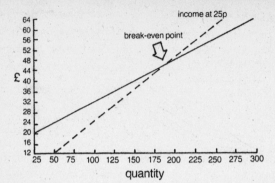

Figure 30

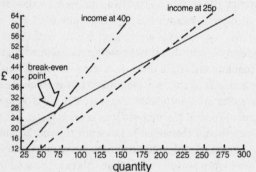

Figure 31

Graphs can deliberately mislead. By changing the scale of one of the axes, a different picture can emerge (see Figure 32).

The purpose of graphs, charts and illustrations in a report is to clarify. There is no place for decoration or misleading information.

Summary

Sometimes words are inadequate if the reader is to visualize what is described.

Photographs, still or moving, can be a great help. But photographs have drawbacks: details can be difficult to see, and shadows can blur outlines.

Diagrams are useful, but they do not show a complete picture.

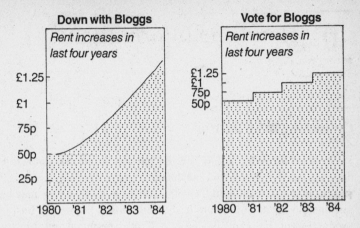

Figure 32

Sometimes a combination of photographs and diagrams needs to be used for adequate communication.

A flow-chart algorithm is a diagram devised to make problem-solving easy. It can be difficult to produce, but if it is carefully designed and clearly laid out, it can be a useful tool.

Pie charts and bar charts are used a great deal, particularly in communicating financial information, as proportions can be seen at a glance.

There are various kinds of technical illustrations. Orthographic and isometric drawings may sometimes be made by authors. Technical illustrations must be drawn by professional technical illustrators. Exploded views, cut-aways, location illustrations and sequences of diagrams can be used to great effect in formal reports.

Most people are familiar with graphs, which convey information simultaneously instead of consecutively in the manner of tables and rows of figures.

Diagrams and illustrations can be misleading or unhelpful. Inaccurate, ambiguous and superfluous illustrations should be avoided in factual writing.

5 Handling Information

Collecting information

What information is collected, and how it is collected, depends largely on the nature of the report, why it is being produced and for whom it is intended. One person, or more than one, may be responsible for its collection. It is essential that the reason for the production of the report is clearly defined. The managing director who asks for a report on absenteeism is going to receive one that is as woolly as his request. Absenteeism where? Among the salaried staff? Among the hourly paid workers? Among men? Among women? In all locations? Over what period? Before embarking on the research for a report, the researcher must have a clear idea of the aim and the intended scope of the investigation.

For the Warnock report, for example, a Committee of Inquiry was established in July 1982 'to examine the social, ethical and legal implications of recent, and potential developments in the field of human assisted reproduction'.

It is also necessary for the terms of reference used in a report to be clearly defined. The report of this Inquiry states in the section entitled 'The General Approach' that two words in the terms of reference need clarifying. One of these is 'embryo'. This is defined as 'the meeting of egg and sperm at fertilization'. The second word is 'potential'. The report explains: 'We took the pragmatic view that we could react only to what we knew, and what we could realistically foresee.' These definitions are essential to the reader's understanding of the information given in the report.

Unless the report deals with classified (confidential) information, it is a good idea to attempt to explain what it is about before beginning to write. Putting ideas into words helps to clarify them.

The material to be collected may come from experimentation, investigation, observation or interviews. The method of research must always be carefully planned with the mandate in view. The data must be relevant and factual. This does not necessarily mean that opinions must be disregarded: those that are based on knowledge and experience can be valuable. But it must be recognized that opinions are not facts.

If experiments are to be conducted, it is assumed that they will be carried out by trained scientists who will design and perform the experiments in an acceptable way. Accuracy is a prime consideration. Results should generally be recorded in words as well as in figures immediately after an experiment is concluded. It is essential for notes to be clearly written and presented so that they can be understood by all readers.

Sometimes a condition or event has to be re-created or simulated for observation or to test a hypothesis (a supposition). This is not always possible. For example, metal fatigue cannot be produced in a certain place in a jumbo jet to find out if it will cause a crash. But a great deal of research has been carried out on the safety of motor cars by examining the effect of crashes on dummies in the cars. This has resulted in an improvement in safety standards. The committee appointed to conduct the inquiry into the Flixborough disaster commissioned experiments to examine the damage to the 20-inch pipe. The tests were designed to 'simulate as closely as possible the behaviour of the original pipe and bellows assembly'. There were a number of uncertainties; none the less, valuable evidence was collected. (See Appendix 1 of the report.) Unfortunately safety recommendations are not always accepted by manufacturers. It is said that an aeroplane fuel can be produced which will not ignite as rapidly as that used today, but it is expensive and for reasons of cost is not used by airlines.

Detailed investigation is vital in the event of a major disaster, particularly if a repetition is to be avoided and/or if large sums of money are involved. Forensic scientists may be called in by insurance companies, to ascertain how a disaster occurred in order to decide which insurance company shall pay. In one large warehouse fire, a forensic scientist was able to discover where the fire started and to prove that it was started by workmen from a repair company called in by the owners of the warehouse. As a result of the report the insurers of the warehouse were saved from paying a very large sum indeed, which had to be paid by the repair company's insurers. This report was the end product of careful observation and forensic investigation aided by detailed photography.

One difficulty that investigators have to face is that of time delay. When a fire has occurred, however quickly the forensic scientist is called in, the fire must be over before forensic investigation can begin. A fire crew will, of necessity, have moved through the building, and possibly police and ambulance staff as well. These will probably be followed by the owners, employees and even sightseers. It would be difficult to claim that nothing has been disturbed, and the validity of the evidence that the forensic scientist is able to collect is affected as a result. In the case of the Flixborough explosion, which took place on 1 June, the people conducting the inquiry were not appointed until 27 June and met for the first time on 2 July. A month passed before the investigation could properly begin. A lot may have happened to the debris in that time.

There are occasions when verbatim reports of, for example, witnesses' evidence are needed. Then either a shorthand writer or a tape-recorder must be used. Interviewing is a skilled technique and is best undertaken by professionals. Unfortunately it is one of those skills that look easy; amateurs think they can do it adequately. If it makes more sense for the report writers or members of the committee to conduct the interviews, they must study the technique. Although it may be advisable for an interview to seem casual, it must be structured.

If informal chat takes the place of an interview, important information may not be unearthed. Suppose that a report is being produced on the communications inside a company and that the mandate is to discover the paths, the methods and the effectiveness of communication, and to make recommendations, if necessary, for improvement. Certain people will be interviewed. If the interviewer begins by saying that the intention is 'to find out all about communications in the company', it is likely that very little will be discovered; the intention is too vague. It must be decided in advance what details are needed. It is useful for the interviewer to write down, in any order, before beginning:

Communication:
From whom? To whom? By what methods?
Official/unofficial (grapevine)?
Upwards/downwards/sideways?

From this a structure of questions can be produced, the answers to which will match the mandate: paths, methods and effectiveness of communications.

It is as well to listen to interviewees' answers to structured questions before prompting because what they leave out is often as important as what they put in. If they do not mention communications from the managing director, these cannot have much significance for them; and if they talk about their communications with the shop stewards but not with the heads of the workforce, a lot can be gathered about communications in the company in general.

It is vitally important that an interviewer's questions are neutral in their tone. An interviewee must never be intimidated or influenced in any way. A question beginning 'Don't you think . . . ?' is unlikely to get a truthful answer. People will often try to give what they think is the expected answer. Factory workers may assume that an interviewer is 'on the boss's side' because of his or her clothes or accent. Above all else, an interviewer must have an open mind.

It is important that the facts that an interviewer is given are disentangled from opinions. Opinions and beliefs are very important, but they must never be confused with facts. Some 300 people and organizations submitted evidence to the Warnock Committee of Inquiry, including representatives of major religious organizations, who would not be expected to hold the same views on such controversial subjects.

Recording data

Data that are collected must be recorded. There are many ways of doing this, and each person will prefer a particular method. If an investigation is carried out by more than one person – for example, a committee or a court of inquiry – then some system of collating the data must be devised. Great care must be taken that what is recorded is what everyone has agreed, and each body will have its own way of making sure that this is so. Sometimes, when the issues are controversial (as, for example, in the Warnock report), some members disassociate themselves from certain findings. Two members of the Warnock report committee expressed dissent from the committee's views on surrogacy, three from the views on the use of human embryos in research and four from one part of those views.

Whichever way of recording data is chosen, the first essential is to decide under what headings the information will be recorded. This will depend on the structure of the investigation.

The most usual (and probably the worst) way of writing down information is on odd pieces of paper (including the proverbial backs of envelopes). If this is done, as it is often convenient to do, then the notes must be transferred to whatever formal system has been devised.

Many people prefer to record data in bound notebooks, as that generally ensures that vital notes will not be mislaid. The drawback of this method is that information is recorded in the order in which it is obtained, which may be entirely haphazard. Obviously this disadvantage can be overcome by having several notebooks for different categories of information, but this technique tends to be cumbersome.

A loose-leaf notebook has the same disadvantage as that of odd pieces of paper in that pages can be mislaid or lost. However, it has the advantage over bound notebooks that information can be moved about to fit into categories and can be rearranged when new information is added. Using differently coloured paper for different subjects is also helpful.

A card-index system can be used in the same way as a loose-leaf notebook, but it is not as portable.

Today a great deal of information is stored in computer memories. The old axiom of 'Garbage in, garbage out' has to be remembered. Advanced technology does not compensate for slovenly or inaccurate data gathering, and the same rules apply to data recording whether it is on paper or in a computer.

Accuracy is of prime importance; information must be recorded when it is available. (That is why the backs of envelopes get used.) Memory, even short-term memory, is fallible. When collecting material for a report one should always carry a notebook and/or a pocket tape-recorder. Where, how and when the information is obtained should also be recorded. However difficult the situation, notes must be legible and figures clearly written, or clearly enunciated if a tape-recorder is used.

A skilled investigator will know how much information to gather. For people less practised it would be helpful if they were to estimate in advance the quantity of data that they will need and the amount of time it will take to collect it.

Classifying data

Collecting, selecting and classifying data are all interrelated. An initial selection must be made while the information is being collected, otherwise an excessive amount of data may accumulate. Classifying the data ensures that it is kept in manageable order and that each separate aspect of the report is covered by sufficient information.

For example, a report on absenteeism among hourly paid workers in one company's factories in three different locations during the periods January to March, April to June, July to September, October to December over the last two years (men and women to be separately assessed) would need to be divided into sections. Location headings would be the first division: London, Birmingham and Manchester. Then these main headings would be subdivided.

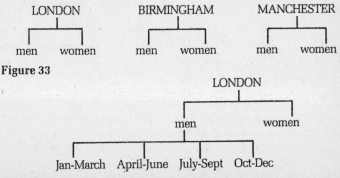

Figure 33

Figure 34

Each subsection would be divided (Figure 34), then divided again (Figure 35). This is an obvious and easy system of classification.

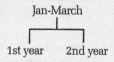

Figure 35

A report on a fire might have the following as its main headings:

> eye-witness reports
> films and photographs
> examination of wreckage
> interviews with owner of premises
> interviews with employees.

The headings under which material is collected may be the same as the headings of the written report but not necessarily. If, in the absenteeism inquiry, it were to emerge that there was a pattern but that it was the same for all locations, then London, Birmingham and Manchester might cease to be main headings.

When material is collected for a report it is obtained chronologically. There is a strong tendency, which must usually be avoided, to present the material also in chronological order. This method of presentation often leaves readers unsure of what the main conclusions are: in fact, it leaves them to do for themselves the most important jobs, which are selecting the data and assessing the importance of conclusions.

When a report is commissioned, the commissioning body must specify the kind of report that is required. If this is not done, the report may turn out to be useless. For example, an employee who is asked merely to 'write a report' on a course on communication may produce an hour-by-hour account.

> We assembled for dinner on Monday night, and were divided into groups. We tried to get to know each others' names, jobs and where we each came from. One man was to be leader or co-ordinator of each group. This was by mutual consent. We were given the itinerary for the course and went away to read it carefully and make notes.
>
> The first lecture was called 'Why communicate?'. The gist was

that as it is wasteful for everyone to re-invent the wheel so to speak, it is better to pass on information about its invention, preferably in a way people can understand, so they can then go away and suggest improvements and applications.

The next lecture was on language. Plain English was advocated, and examples were given of jargon and gobbledegook, both of which inhibit understanding.

After dinner we had a workshop session where we could make visual aids for a talk we each had to give the next day, to communicate to our fellow students what our jobs involved.

After breakfast we each gave our talks, using the visual aids we had made the night before.

And so on . . . . This kind of report would be virtually useless, and in these circumstances it would be better to use a prepared form of multiple-choice questions, which asks the respondent to simply tick the answer preferred or provides spaces where questions can be answered in a few words.

Reaching conclusions

The producer of a report must know when to stop. This may be decided by someone else. For example, the managing director may say that a requested report on absenteeism must be completed in a month's time. 'As soon as possible' is a common request, which leaves it to the producer to decide. Sometimes the nature of an inquiry means that it could go on indefinitely, and an arbitrary stopping-point must be fixed. Probably the Warnock report is in this category.

The mandate must be kept constantly in mind, and every effort must be made to reach the most correct conclusion possible. The results of a conclusion may be far-reaching. If metal fatigue is diagnosed as the reason for a jumbo-jet crash, then every one of that particular type and age of aircraft must be examined or even grounded, with resultant chaos for travellers and financial loss to the airline. If a report of a motor accident shows that the steering of a car is liable to malfunction, then all cars of that particular model must be called in for examination and possible adaptation. If a forensic scientist produces incontrovertible evidence of when and how a fire that destroyed a factory started, millions of pounds in compensation may have to be paid. Sometimes the report of an inquiry can damage or destroy someone's reputation and career. If 'pilot error' caused a plane to crash, all the evidence must be produced to prove beyond doubt that this really was the case.

In Chapter 2, I discussed whether complete objectivity is possible, and the answer was that it is very difficult to achieve. Obviously all experimental, mathematical and statistical evidence must be checked and double-checked to eliminate error and to prevent false and possibly damaging conclusions being drawn.

Selecting data

Even more than when collecting material, when selecting what is to be included in a report it is essential to keep in mind those for whom the report is intended. Some writers of reports get so carried away by the subject that they fail to see the wood for the trees. An enormous number of mathematical calculations, essential to the conclusions of a report, may totally confuse the non-mathematical reader. Where specialized knowledge is required readers need to feel that they can rely on the conclusions of the experts. Certainly they need to understand the arguments but rarely every scientific detail. This is true of the Flixborough report.

A non-expert should feel safe in relying on Professor Davidson, for example, as the letters after his name (M A, Ph D, Sc D, F R S, C Eng, F I Chem E, and M I Mech E) indicate that he is highly educated and particularly knowledgeable about chemical engineering; the F R S in particular shows that he has contributed much to the world's knowledge. However, we all know that experts can draw different conclusions from the same evidence, so enough detail must be given for the reader to understand and be convinced of the report's validity. This was done in the Flixborough report when the 8-inch hypothesis was abandoned in favour of the 20-inch hypothesis.

One reason why report writers may be tempted to include too much information for their readership is because they want their hard work to be acknowledged. This is particularly so if someone in a company is asked to produce a report for a superior or for the board of directors. But the length of a report is not a measure of how much work has gone into its production. After all, a great deal of time was spent by a number of people on producing the fifty-one pages of the Flixborough report as well as the ninety-four pages of the Warnock report.

Not only must the readership be kept in mind but also the purpose of the report. The aim is not just to hold an inquest but to enable some action to be taken if this proves to be necessary. For example, to know why a disaster occurred can help to avoid its repetition. To apportion blame may be necessary – although useless from most points of view – but the prevention of another jumbo-jet crash or factory explosion may be the main aim of an inquiry and its subsequent report. A report on absenteeism would be produced in the hope that a pattern might emerge: whether absenteeism was the same in all locations, for example, or the same for male and female employees. From the results steps could be taken to reduce the amount of absenteeism. It might simply be discovered that the factory's absentee figures were the same as the national average.

Reports such as the Warnock report are intended not to examine the cause of a disaster (as was the case at Flixborough) or to combat industrial problems (such as the one on absenteeism) but to make recommendations to the government about issues that have come to be of national importance. The famous education reports of the last thirty years or so – Crowther, Plowden, Robbins and Newsom – have been of this kind, and such reports must be comprehensible to a very wide readership because their subject is the concern of the general public rather than of individuals or companies.

Having reached his or her conclusions the writer must decide what must be in the report to substantiate these conclusions. At this stage it is not necessary to decide how the report shall be presented – whether it will be short, with various appendices, for example, or whether the evidence will be included in the general text. The first step is to decide which parts of the information are to be used. The fact that three experiments failed because they were wrongly designed may indicate that the experimenter was industrious if nothing else but is of no interest to the reader of the report. How many visits to London, Birmingham and Manchester were made to investigate absenteeism is irrelevant. What matters is what was discovered on those visits. Dropping the results of a lot of labour into the waste-paper basket is hard, but it is often necessary, and may lead to a less wasteful expenditure of time in subsequent investigations.

By this stage, the data have been collected and classified, conclusions have been reached and everything that is of no consequence has been rejected. The next major consideration, taking into account who must and who will read the report when it is published, is how the report is to be structured.

Summary

Collecting data What material must be collected for a report depends on its purpose and the readers for whom it is intended. The purpose of the report and its terms of reference must be clearly defined, and if they are not, the report writer must ask for clarification. Explaining the report and its aims to someone else can help the writer to sort out his or her ideas.

There are various ways of collecting information: by experiment, investigation, observation and interviewing. Data must be relevant to the mandate and must be factual. Opinions should be treated cautiously but not necessarily ignored. Accuracy is most important. Sometimes a situation or condition must be re-created to test a hypothesis, although this is not always possible.

Interviewing is a special technique, which must be mastered. The interview must be structured so that the questions produce the kind of information that is required. The interviewer's opinions or prejudices must never influence the shape of the questions.

Recording data Information that has been collected can be recorded in various ways. in bound notebooks, loose-leaf notebooks and card indexes, on tapes and in computer memories. It is essential to record data under headings or in categories. For the sake of accuracy, information should be recorded at the time that it becomes available. Where, how and when it is obtained should also be recorded. Photographs can be of great help in some circumstances.

Classifying data It is necessary to classify the data that are obtained. Main headings will probably be chosen, but these may change during the course of the investigation.

There is a danger that material collected chronologically may be presented in the same way: generally, this should be avoided.

Reaching conclusions The report writer must know when to stop collecting data and to reach some conclusions. These conclusions must be supported by sufficient evidence. Not only large sums of money but also people's lives and reputations may depend on the accuracy of these findings.

Selecting data When selecting which material is to be included in the report, the readership must be constantly kept in mind. Data that will confuse or that are not necessary to support the conclusions should be rigorously cut. The readers should be able to rely on the expertise of those who are selected to produce the report. However, enough evidence must be supplied to convince readers that the conclusions are valid. The purpose of the report and the possible results of the findings must also be borne in mind.

6 The Structure of a Report

The structure of a report has two aspects, which can perhaps be described as *external* and *internal*. The external structure is the formal framework that you devise for your summary, findings and conclusions, so that readers can find their way about your report quickly and easily. The internal structure is the means by which you assemble and present the information that you have gathered, sentence by sentence, paragraph by paragraph, until you have constructed a logical, coherent edifice.

The simplest kind of report to produce, from the point of view of both external and internal structure, is the pre-printed form on which standard questions require answers. Such a form may not always be appropriate, however. If, for example, a parked car had been dented by a lorry driver who left a note saying that the accident was his fault, it would be irrelevant for the owner of the car, who was not even present at the time, to be asked later for the date on which he passed his driving test (a standard question on accident report forms). Report forms are most constructive when they require answers only to those questions that are relevant to a particular case. And, of course, every report, no matter how simple, must draw conclusions.

Even if your report is little more than a memorandum to your boss, it must have a logical structure – for example, what you were asked to report on, how you have gone about the task, what you have discovered and your recommendations (if those were requested). In addition you may want to append information that, though not central to your discussion, may be useful to readers. Suppose that your report mentions interviews with twenty people; you may choose to list their names on a separate page at the end of the report in case their identities help to throw light on any of your findings. By structuring your report in this way, you are able to provide extra information that may be illuminating and to ensure that non-essential details do not obscure the main issues of the report.

External structure – the formal framework

There is no standard structure of a report (though some large organizations lay down their own rules about structure, a procedure that is sensible only if the reports they ask for, and receive, are all of the same type). Let us look at the structure of three different reports.

The Flixborough report was structured under these headings:

Introduction
Scope of the investigation
Site and general history of Flixborough Works
Layout of the works
Organization of the Company
Section 25A [the site of the explosion] – The process and layout
Start up procedures
Events from 28 March to 1 April
Events from 29 May to explosion
The explosion and aftermath
The problem stated
Two-stage rupture of the by-pass [the two-stage hypothesis]
Eye-witness, film and photographic evidence*
The 8-inch hypothesis
Examination of individual steps in 8-inch hypothesis
General observations on the 8-inch hypothesis
Damage connected with the 8-inch line
20-inch and 8-inch hypotheses compared
Miscellaneous: (a) Security (b) Safety precautions generally (c) Storage of potentially dangerous substances
Lessons to be learned [specific, general, miscellaneous]

[*This ends with an examination of the 20-inch hypothesis.]

Matters to be referred to the special committee or other
bodies
Summary
Costs
Acknowledgements
Appendix 1 Experimental evidence relating to rupture of
20-inch pipe
Appendix 2 Damage to 8-inch pipe – metallurgical inves-
tigations
Appendix 3 Procedural history
Appendix 4 List of representations
Appendix 5 List of witnesses
Appendix 6 Reports

This can be summarized:

what happened
the problem stated
the two-stage hypothesis – quickly rejected
evidence from eye-witnesses and film
the 8-inch hypothesis – examined in detail and rejected
the 20-inch hypothesis – compared with the 8-inch and
accepted
lessons to be learned
summary
information not in the body of the report.

This is evidently a logical structure: what happened, the need to
discover why, three possibilities examined in order of probability
(resulting in the first two being rejected and the third accepted),
what should be learned from it and a summary. The report proper
(from the Introduction to the Summary), which is clear to any non-
scientific reader, is only thirty-seven pages long. There are also
seventeen photographs and eleven diagrams, which are integral
parts of the report. All the additional information is in appendices,
which the reader may or may not choose to read. These take up
eleven pages.

The Warnock report is divided into chapters, with additional sections:

1.   The general approach
2.   Infertility: the scope and organization of services
3.   Techniques for the alleviation of infertility: common threads
4–8. Various techniques for the alleviation of infertility
9.   The wider use of these techniques
10. The freezing and storage of human semen, eggs and embryos
11. Human embryos and research
12. Possible future developments in research
13. Regulating infertility services and research
     List of recommendations
     Expressions of dissent
     Appendix: List of those submitting evidence
     Index

Again, a perfectly logical structure. In this report the reader can assume that all the members of the Committee of Inquiry agreed with what is written, except where expressions of dissent are recorded. As well as the 300 organizations that submitted evidence, 695 letters and submissions from the public were received; this fact is stated in the appendix. The main body of the report comprises ninety-four pages. The only additional information is the list of people who submitted evidence, which could not be included in the text.

A structure similar to that of the Flixborough report, but different in its balance, is found in the following report on herbicides, the mandate of which was 'to consider . . . whether there is any sound medical or scientific evidence that humans or other living creatures, or our environment would come to any harm if certain cleared herbicides continue to be used in this country for the recommended purposes and in the recommended way'. The report is presented as follows:

Chapter 1   Background to the report
             A The last report
             B Main developments since the last report

Chapter 2   Appraisal of evidence
                   A Case studies
                   B Animal data
                   C Human exposure
                   D The environment
                   E Safety
                   F Alternatives
                   G International comparisons
Chapter 3   Conclusions

This is the report, comprising nineteen pages. There follow nine appendices, which contain all the back-up material for the three chapters. These take up thirty-seven pages. The appendices are followed by a glossary and a short note on terms.

This structure is admirable. Those who simply want to know the conclusions of the inquiry need to read only nineteen pages, but all the information on which the conclusions are based is in the appendices for those who want further details of any or every section of each chapter.

Placing a glossary at the end of a report is satisfactory if the contents page states where the glossary is to be found. Otherwise the reader may spend time trying to discover elsewhere the definitions of unfamiliar terms, only to find at the end of the report that that time has been wasted.

The components of the formal framework

The most usual structure of a report is probably:

title page
list of contents
summary
introduction
main text
conclusions
recommendations
appendices

with acknowledgements, a glossary, references and a bibliography where these are appropriate.

Title page   The purpose of the title page is to tell the reader what the report is about. Some reports, particularly in-company ones, will have only a pre-determined readership, in which case the title should simply define the scope of the investigation. For example, if a report on absenteeism in three locations is to be read by the main board of a company, the boards of the three locations, and certain other interested people, the title page might read:

A Report
Absenteeism in XYZ Limited
in London, Birmingham and Manchester
1984–1986

Most governmental reports carry the name of the chairperson. The Warnock report is commonly known by the chairwoman's name rather than as the *Report of the Committee of Inquiry into Human Fertilization and Embryology*. Occasionally, however, a different kind of title is used. One famous report was made by the Central Advisory Council for Education at the request of the Minister for Education and was submitted in 1963. The chairman was John Newsom. The purpose of the report and the terms of reference were 'To consider the education between the ages of 13 and 16 of pupils of average or less than average ability who are or will be following full-time courses either at schools or in establishments of further education. The term education shall be understood to include extra-curricular activities.' This could have been titled *The Education, between the Ages of 13 and 16, of Pupils of Average or Less than Average Ability*. Instead it was called *Half Our Future*, which, it must be agreed, is a more arresting title.

List of contents   A table of contents is essential for a report of more than a few pages as it provides a guide for the reader. It is particularly helpful in the absence of a summary.

Where there is a table of contents, an index is probably unnecessary except in a very long report. There is no index at the end of the

Flixborough or herbicide report, but there is one at the end of the Warnock report, perhaps because this report deals with so many different aspects of infertility and possible alleviations that interested readers may want to refer to particular pages and paragraphs.

Summary   The summary, if one is included, can serve a double purpose. It is there for the person who only wants an outline of the report and it serves as a précis for those who have read, or will read, the whole report. In some cases the summary can act as a conclusion, as it is a condensed version of the main body of the report.

The summary must, of necessity, be written after the report and must match its structure. No material may be introduced that is not in the main body of the report. As the summary is written last, there is a temptation to include afterthoughts, but this must be avoided. If the afterthoughts are of some significance, then the main body of the report must be revised. One of the advantages of drafting a summary is that it may draw attention to something that is missing from, or an illogicality in, the report.

It is for the author of the report to decide whether the summary shall be placed at the beginning or the end unless the report is being written for an organization that has a standard structure. If this is not the case, then the author's decision must be based on a knowledge of the potential readership: if a substantial number will want simply to read the summary, it should be at the front; but if most readers will read the whole report, it should be at the end.

The summary of the Flixborough report, which comes at the end, is worth quoting in full.

Summary
225   Our main conclusions may be summarized as follows:
(i) The scene was set for disaster at Flixborough when, at the end of March 1974, one of the reactors in the cyclohexane oxidation train on the plant was removed owing to the development of a leak, and the gap between the flanking reactors bridged by an inadequately supported bypass assembly consisting of a 20-inch dog-leg pipe between two expansion bellows. (See paragraphs 53–73.)
(ii) The fact that the bridging of the gap presented engineering design problems was not appreciated by anyone at Nypro with

the result that there was no proper design study, no proper consideration of the need for support, no safety testing, no reference to the relevant British Standard and no reference to the bellows manufacturer's 'Designers Guide'. (See paragraphs 56–63.)

(iii) As a result of the above omissions, responsibility for which was very properly admitted by Nypro at an early stage, the assembly as installed was liable to rupture at pressures well below safety valve pressure, and at or below operating temperature. (See paragraphs 124–128.)

(iv) The integrity of a well designed and constructed plant was thereby destroyed and, although no-one was aware of it, disaster might have occurred at any time thereafter.

(v) The blame for the defects in the design, support and testing of the bypass must be shared between the many individuals concerned, at and below Board level but it should be made plain that no blame attaches to those whose task was fabrication and installation. They carried out the work, which they had been asked to do, properly and carefully. As between individuals it is not for us to apportion blame.

(vi) On the 1st June 1974 the assembly was subjected to conditions for pressure and temperature more severe than any which had previously prevailed but no higher than careful and conscientious plant operators could be expected to permit. For the attainment of such pressures and temperatures none of the Control Room staff at the time can be criticized much less blamed. (See paragraph 87.)

(vii) The more severe conditions of pressure and temperature were sufficient to and did cause the assembly to rupture, and thus to release large quantities of cyclohexane. Such cyclohexane formed a cloud of vapour (mixed with air) which exploded. (See paragraph 6.)

(viii) The alternative theory which was advanced before us, namely that the assembly failed as a result of a small external explosion following prior rupture of a nearby 8-inch line, although superficially credible, proved on detailed examination to be founded on a sequence of improbabilities and coincidences so great as to leave us in no doubt that it should be rejected. There was, in our judgment, no prior explosion. (See paragraph 191.)

226 We have not included in the above summary any mention of lessons to be learned for we have dealt with this in detail very recently in this Report. (See paragraphs 195–216.) We believe, however, that if the steps which we have recommended are carried out, the risk of any similar disaster, already remote, will be lessened. We use the phrase 'already remote' advisedly for we

wish to make it plain that we found nothing to suggest that the plant as originally designed and constructed created any unacceptable risk. The disaster was caused wholly by the coincidence of a number of unlikely errors in the design and installation of a modification. Such a combination of errors is very unlikely ever to be repeated. Our recommendations should ensure that no similar combination occurs again and that even if it should do so, the errors would be detected before any serious consequences ensued.

Introduction   As its name implies, this part of the report is to introduce or set the scene. Therefore, it should say what the report is about. The introduction to the Flixborough report does just that. It begins:

> At about 4.53 p.m. on Saturday 1st June 1974 the Flixborough Works of Nypro (UK) Limited (Nypro) were virtually demolished by an explosion of warlike dimensions. Of those working on the site at the time, 28 were killed and 36 others suffered injuries. If the explosion had occurred on an ordinary working day, many more people would have been on the site, and the number of casualties would have been much greater. Outside the Works, injuries and damage were widespread but no-one was killed. Fifty-three people were recorded as casualties by the casualty bureau which was set up by the police; hundreds more suffered relatively minor injuries which were not recorded. Property damage extended over a wide area, and a preliminary survey showed that 1,821 houses and 167 shops and factories had suffered to a greater or lesser degree.

It goes on to say how and when the people who were to hold the investigation were appointed and to note that an interim report had been prepared earlier by Her Majesty's Factory Inspectorate, that other people were also investigating the incident and that a large number of reports were prepared, of which a list is included in an appendix.

The introduction to the herbicide report sets the scene by briefly reviewing the general nature and substance of the report previous to it. This exercise is particularly relevant when a report is one of a series and will be read by those who have read earlier reports and will need to be reminded of them and, in some cases, by new readers who need to be put in the picture.

The introduction to the Warnock report is called 'Foreword' and it clearly states the aim of the Inquiry and the attitude of the members towards it: 'a steady and general point of view' was the guiding principle.

The importance of the introduction is that it should prepare the reader for what follows. It is essential that nothing in the body of the report should be incomprehensible as a result of the omission of vital preliminary information.

The main text   It is obvious that, if it is of any length, the body of the report will have a structure of its own. How the material collected has been classified and how the conclusions have been arrived at will dictate this structure. The argument must be developed in a logical way; the reasoning must be clear to the readers; and the evidence submitted to support the conclusions must be relevant.

The author must decide how much information to put in the body of the report and how much to put in appendices. From the examples given it can be seen that this balance varies.

The Flixborough report	Text: 38 pages including 17 photographs and 11 diagrams
	Appendices: 11 pages
The Warnock report	Text: 94 pages
	A list of people who submitted evidence
The herbicide report	Text: 19 pages
	Appendices: 37 pages

The body of the report may contain conclusions. This is so in the Flixborough report, where three hypotheses are examined, two of them rejected and the third accepted. There is no section headed 'Conclusions', but they appear in the summary, which begins, 'Our main conclusions may be summarized . . .'

Conclusions   Although the conclusions may appear either in the main body of the report or in the summary, some reports have a section headed 'Conclusions'. The herbicide report is one of these, and the first paragraph of this section is unequivocal:

> What we have had to consider in this Review is whether there is
> any sound medical or scientific evidence that humans or other
> living creatures, or our environment, would come to any harm if
> certain cleared herbicides continue to be used in this country for
> the recommended purposes and in the recommended way. We
> have found none.

As in the summary (which, as I have pointed out, may serve
instead of a conclusion), no new idea or fact must be introduced that
is not dealt with in the body of the text. It should consist of unquali-
fied statements. The reader should be quite clear that this is the end
of the report. The conclusion should conclude.

Recommendations   Although the conclusion should not introduce
new ideas or facts, recommendations may be incorporated in this
section. Otherwise they can be presented separately. Recommendations can be thought of as 'lessons to be learned' as they are called in
the Flixborough report. The main conclusion in this case is that 'the
disaster was caused by the introduction into a well designed and
constructed plant of a modification which destroyed its integrity.'
The consequent recommendation is, 'The immediate lesson to be
learned is that measures must be taken to ensure that the technical
integrity of the plant is not violated.' There follows advice as to how
this can be achieved.

Appendices   These provide a way of presenting detailed information that, if put in the main body of the report, would either give
more information than some readers require or interrupt the flow of
the narrative to the detriment of the logical exposition of the investigation. Once more, if the author of the report always bears in mind
the readership, it will help to determine what shall go into the main
body of the report and what shall be put into appendices.

Sometimes there are no appendices, and readers must accept that
the investigators have taken into account all the information at their
disposal in order to reach the conclusions that they have set out. A
report can become enormously long if all the evidence that has been
submitted is included.

Acknowledgements   By the nature of any report, the author will have received help. It may be from a few people or it may be from many: in the Warnock report 300 organizations submitted evidence and 695 letters were received. All assistance needs acknowledgement, if only generally. If one person or several have been particularly helpful, they deserve special thanks. Acknowledgements should be placed at the beginning of a report. They should not be forgotten.

References and bibliography References give bibliographical details of books, journals or papers from which extracts have been quoted or that have been specifically mentioned in the text. A bibliography consists of additional reading matter that may supplement parts of the text. References are listed in the order in which the books or journals are referred to in the text. A bibliography should be listed alphabetically by author.

References and a bibliography are of value only if they enable would-be readers to buy a book or journal or to find it in a library; therefore precise details must be given. A reference for a book begins with the forename or initials of the author and the surname; these are followed by the exact title of the book, the edition, the publisher and, finally, the date of publication. The title of the book is printed in italic.

> Vernon Booth, *Communicating in Science*, Cambridge University Press, 1984
> H. W. Fowler, *A Dictionary of Modern English Usage*, 2nd edition, Oxford University Press, 1985

If these two books were cited in a bibliography, the order of the surname and first name or initials would be reversed.

Journals are often put together in volumes, usually one for each year. It is helpful to put the numbers of the relevant pages. The publisher's name is not put on periodicals. It is customary to print the name of the article in roman type and the journal in italic. The number of the volume is printed in bold type, followed by the year and then the page number or numbers.

| N. R. F. Maier, | 'An aspect of human reasoning', *Journal of Psychology*, **24** (1933), 144–155 |
| G. H. Hers, | 'Making Science a Good Read', *Nature*, **307** (1984), 205 |

If a volume is paginated as a whole rather than each of its issues being paginated separately, the issue number must be given after the volume number. These two can be distinguished by using arabic numerals for the volume and roman for the issue.

Care must be taken with references, particular for journals. It is extremely irritating to be directed to volume 121 only to discover, after much research, that it is volume 112 that you need.

Scientific and technical books, unless they are meant for the general reader, are not usually to be found in public libraries. Libraries of universities, faculties, colleges and technical and scientific institutions are more likely to contain them. The three copyright libraries, which are the University Library in Cambridge, the Bodleian in Oxford and the library of the British Museum in London, are supposed to contain every book published in the United Kingdom, but it is not always easy to obtain copies.

The internal structure of a report

A report's internal structure is the invisible grid that helps you to marshal your thoughts coherently and to present your findings and conclusions in a logical order. It is easier to construct something and to use it if pieces are presented in the right order rather than in a haphazard heap. (Anyone who has tried to assemble, for example, a kitchen cabinet that has been delivered in pieces will know about this, particularly if the 'simple' instructions provided by the maker turn out to be not so simple after all.)

The human mind uses various devices for acquiring, arranging and remembering information. Making shapes and patterns is one of these devices. The difficulty is that many of the patterns and relationships that we make are personal to us. Most people have played the free-association game. You say, 'Grass,' and I reply, 'Horse,' because a horse was discovered on my lawn this morning; someone else replies, 'Lawnmower,' because he has been nagged about not cutting the grass. The lesson to be learned from this is that it is unwise to expect other people to see the same relationships and patterns as you do: they must be made explicit. It is the duty of the author of a report to make it as easy as possible for the reader to assimilate the information it contains by following a clear and objective line of reasoning.

One way of structuring the report would be to start by presenting all the evidence. This is where the investigation began, so perhaps the report's readers should start in the same place.

Suppose each box in Figure 36(a) to be a piece of evidence that has been collected. When the author of the report considers these, they should be arranged in groups (see Figure 36(b)) so that the weight of evidence can be assessed and conclusions drawn.

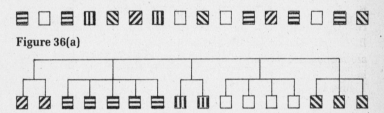

Figure 36(a)

Figure 36(b)

The *gathering* of information is like making a shopping list; the *presentation* of that information is like rearranging the items on your shopping list according to the supermarket section in which they can be found or the shops in which they can be bought. Given a logical arrangement, you can plan the shortest – and therefore the most efficient – shopping trip (see Figures 37 and 38).

Even if a report is fully comprehensible to every possible reader, it is not always feasible to include in it all the evidence that was collected. It is the duty of the person or committee conducting the investigation to examine an enormous amount of evidence and to present the report as a summary of that evidence. The Warnock report is an example. Imagine what the size of the report would have been if the entire content of the 300 presentations and 695 letters had been printed. The report is itself a summary, which explains why there is no section called 'Summary' within it.

Shopping-list

bacon
eggs
tomatoes
coffee
bread
milk.

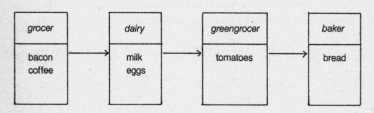

grocer	dairy	greengrocer	baker
bacon coffee	milk eggs	tomatoes	bread

Figure 37

Figure 37 is a more efficient arrangement than Figure 38.

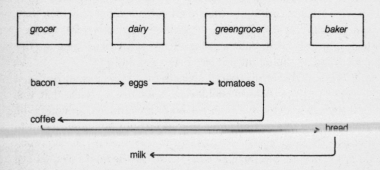

Figure 38

A report is always the answer to a question. What steps should the government take to regulate the various ways of overcoming infertility? Will using a certain herbicide be a danger to human beings and other living creatures? What caused the fire in the kitchen of 18 Romsey Avenue? Why did a particular jumbo jet crash?

To answer the main question, other questions have to be asked. Let us examine the Flixborough report from this angle: how can another explosion at a chemical plant like Flixborough be prevented?

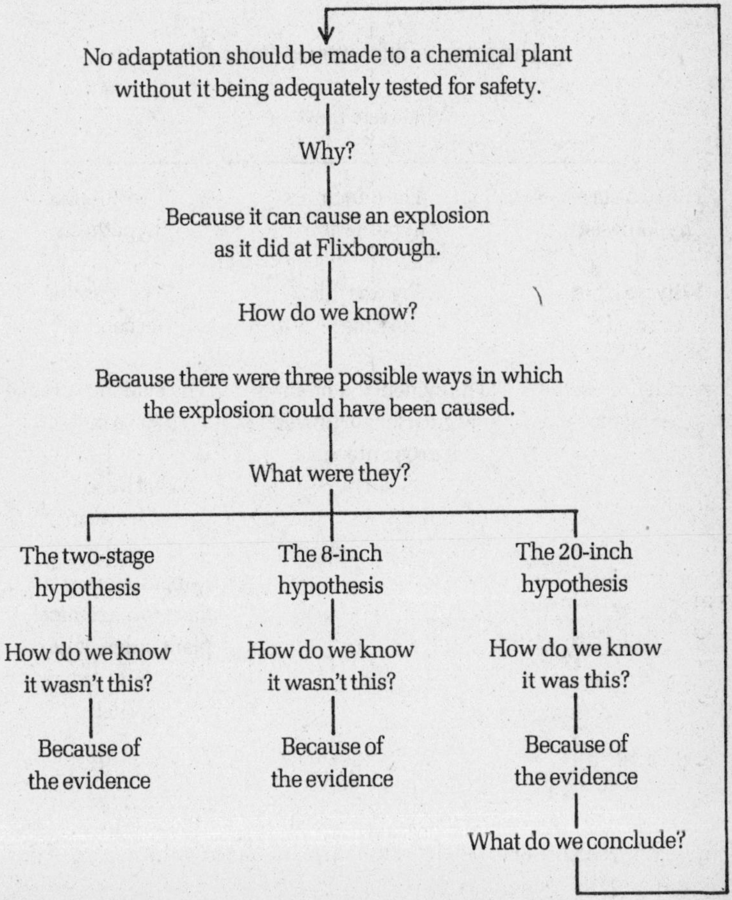

No adaptation should be made to a chemical plant without it being adequately tested for safety.

Why?

Because it can cause an explosion as it did at Flixborough.

How do we know?

Because there were three possible ways in which the explosion could have been caused.

What were they?

The two-stage hypothesis	The 8-inch hypothesis	The 20-inch hypothesis
How do we know it wasn't this?	How do we know it wasn't this?	How do we know it was this?
Because of the evidence	Because of the evidence	Because of the evidence

What do we conclude?

Figure 39

We could start with a simple statement (a conclusion) and consider questions that might arise naturally from it. In fact, the report can be seen as a kind of conversation: the writer must anticipate and resolve a series of questions that he imagines readers will ask.

Instead of beginning with a statement or conclusion, one could start with the first question that might be asked:

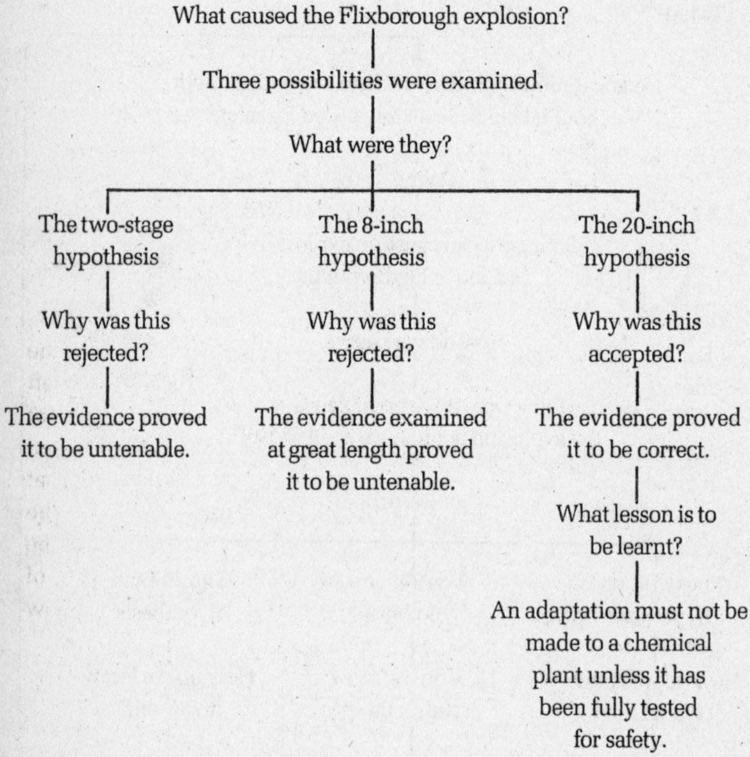

What caused the Flixborough explosion?

Three possibilities were examined.

What were they?

The two-stage hypothesis	The 8-inch hypothesis	The 20-inch hypothesis
Why was this rejected?	Why was this rejected?	Why was this accepted?
The evidence proved it to be untenable.	The evidence examined at great length proved it to be untenable.	The evidence proved it to be correct.

What lesson is to be learnt?

An adaptation must not be made to a chemical plant unless it has been fully tested for safety.

Figure 40

As we have seen, answering the questions that any report raises involves a selection procedure, which is dictated by the nature of the report and the readership.

The questions and answers have upwards, downwards and sideways relationships. Whether one moves upwards or downwards in the presentation of the report can be a matter of choice, although it is probably best to move downwards from the question to the conclusion. Certainly in the investigation and production of the report the only way to move is from the collection of data to the answer to the main question. A sideways relationship exists between levels of equal importance. The three hypotheses in the Flixborough report are on the same level, as are the three results of the examination of all the evidence (see Figure 41).

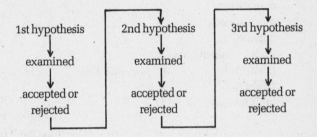

Figure 41

Earlier it was said that if the detailed evidence is beyond the understanding of the majority of readers, then it might as well be left out. In this case, it can be, and often is, put in appendices. In terms of structure this means that one line of the horizontal structure is taken out of the main body of the report to be placed elsewhere. What matters is that the logic of the structure is maintained and that the levels of reasoning are clear, although within these levels it may be necessary to proceed vertically at some points. Whatever the line of argument, however, the reader of the report must be able to follow the reasoning stage by stage.

Summary

Every report, long or short, must have a clear and logical external and internal structure. The author must consider carefully the purpose of the report, its probable length and its eventual readership.

There is no standard external structure: this chapter has examined three reports that were organized in different ways, the Flixborough report, the Warnock report and a report on herbicides. There are, however, standard components that form the framework of a report. These are:

> title page
> list of contents
> summary
> introduction
> main text
> conclusions
> recommendations
> appendices
> acknowledgements ⎫
> glossary   ⎬ as appropriate
> references   ⎪
> bibliography   ⎭

A report is always the answer to a question, which has itself raised other questions. The report can be regarded as a series of questions and answers, organized in a logical sequence. It is essential that the writer should maintain a coherent line of argument whatever external structure has been selected for the presentation of the information. The writer must also be aware of, and guard against, the influence of subjective reasoning, which may obscure the arguments and the conclusions of the report.

7 Style

There is more to writing than observing the rules of grammar and syntax, avoiding gobbledegook, using jargon only in reports that have a specialized readership, keeping sentences short, and striving towards plain English. There is something called 'style'. This is a word that is very difficult to define.

When the word 'style' is applied to writing, it refers mostly to what is individual, what distinguishes one person's writing from another's. It will be obvious to most people that there is a difference in style between the two examples quoted below. That they were written within a year of each other is important, as differences in style can sometimes be related to different stages in history, and, therefore, to fashion. The first is the beginning of *The Rainbow* by D. H. Lawrence, first published in 1915:

> The Brangwens had lived for generations on the Marsh Farm, in the meadows where the Erewash twisted sluggishly through alder trees, separating Derbyshire from Nottinghamshire. Two miles away, a church-tower stood on a hill, the houses of the little country town climbing assiduously up to it.

The second is the beginning of *A Portrait of the Artist as a Young Man* by James Joyce, first published in 1916:

> Once upon a time and a very good time it was there was a moocow coming down along the road and this moocow that was coming down along the road met a nicens little boy named baby tuckoo . . .
>
> His father told him that story: his father looked at him through a glass: he had a hairy face.
>
> He was baby tuckoo. The moocow came down the road where Betty Byrne lived: she sold lemon platt.

To analyse the differences in style between Lawrence and Joyce would be out of place here, as we are concerned not with literary style but with communication. Style is important in the writing of reports, as it will affect the ease with which they can be read and understood.

The smallest part of the structure of a report is the putting together of words: the sentence. Very little can go wrong with the simple subject-and-verb sentence:

> The factory has closed.
> The turnover will double.
> The temperature is high.

But using very short sentences like these leads to awkward and childish writing, which is irritating to read.

Once sentences become more complicated troubles can begin; care must be taken with style. Word order matters since in English different sequences of words, without being incorrect, can change emphasis, if not sense.

In the following example, the change in word order results in a change of emphasis.

> His condition is still serious but is improving.
> His condition is improving but is still serious.

However, a change in word order can alter the meaning of a sentence.

> He **only** reads on *Wednesdays.*
> *(His only activity is reading.)*
>
> He reads **only** on Wednesdays.
> *(He does not read on any other day.)*

Very short sentences, although they have the advantage of being easy to understand, are irritating to read if several of them follow each other. At the other end of the scale is the very long sentence in which the reader gets lost, such as the following sentence from a pensions document.

> For the purposes of this part of the schedule a person over pen-
> sionable age, not being an insured person, shall be treated as an
> employed person if he would be an insured person were he under
> pensionable age and would be an employed person were he an
> insured person.

I doubt if that sentence means anything to anybody. It reminds one of
the old story of Robert Browning, who, when asked what some lines
in one of his poems meant, said: 'When I wrote that, only God and
Robert Browning knew what it meant. Now, only God knows.'

While choosing that sentence to illustrate the problem of getting
lost, I read a large number of sentences that at first seemed incomprehensible, but that made sense after a second reading. In a report
the author should not expect the reader to read every sentence twice
to extract the meaning. Try out what you have written on someone
who is not familiar with the subject, or who has the same amount of
knowledge as the reader of the report will have.

Sentences are grouped into paragraphs. Once more we come back
to structure. The paragraph, as H. W. Fowler has pointed out in
Modern English Usage, is a unit of thought, and not of length. Each
paragraph should deal with one subject or one aspect of a subject.
There is a tendency in present-day writing, especially present-day
journalism, to make each sentence a paragraph. Certainly solid
blocks of print are off-putting, but if the writer of a report has considered his structure, then paragraphs, containing units of thought,
are an important part of that structure. If the writer has said all that
there is to say about a certain point, then a new paragraph should be
started even if the previous one is short. Two short paragraphs must
not be joined up to make one longer one, as this is confusing to the
reader, who expects one unit of thought but finds two and wonders if
there has been a mistake. On the other hand a very long paragraph
may be divided into two if there is a convenient break in the logic of
the thought.

The layout of reports will be considered in a later chapter, but it is
worth mentioning that government reports are often presented in
consecutively numbered paragraphs.

One of the peculiarities from which report writers suffer is called
pseudo-objectivity, which is achieved by using the impersonal
passive:

It is believed that . . .
It is established that . . .
It has been shown that . . .
It is proposed that . . .

It is called pseudo-objectivity because the report writer has avoided saying 'I' or 'we' because 'I believe' or 'we believe' sounds like a subjective judgement (particularly 'I believe'). If it is the writer who believes, or has established, or has shown, or is proposing, then this should be made plain. If the report is the work of more than one person, then of course the 'I' becomes 'we'. If someone other than the writer is the originator of the belief or fact, then this should be said directly:

Hindus believe that . . .   *not*   It is believed by Hindus . . .

Smith and Jones established that . . .   *not*   It was established by Smith and Jones . . .

Just as unnecessary and irritating as never saying 'I' or 'we' is the opposite fault: the excessive use of 'I'. There are occasions when you are writing on behalf of a whole organization, even if the report is all your own work, and then it is better to say 'we', or use the name of the company or organization.

One difficulty a report writer meets is needing to use the same word over and over again. If you are writing about structure, for example, and that word appears in every sentence, the report does not read well. It is worth taking time to avoid repetition as much as possible. A thesaurus can be useful, but it seldom has an exact synonym of the word it is to replace. In *Roget's Thesaurus* the synonyms for 'structure' are: 'organization', 'pattern', 'plan', 'complex', 'shape', 'frame'. None of these contains the idea of building-up something, although 'organization' could sometimes be used.

A peculiar disease from which some writers of formal documents suffer is the inability to use an ordinary word instead of a less ordinary one. They live in residences, not houses, for example, and they commence rather than begin or start. Here are some of the more common of these words and their simple equivalents:

acquiesce	agree
adhere	stick
ameliorate	improve
enhance	
ascertain	find out
assist	help
cogitate	think
endeavour	try
frequently	often
initiate	begin
request	ask
necessitate	need
reside	live
terminate	end
utilize	use

Similarly, writers often use several words where one will do:

blue in colour
square in shape
first of all
small in size
falling down
it is clear that
at this moment in time
the true facts are

Using ordinary words and avoiding unnecessary ones makes for good style in report writing, and good style makes for easy reading and helps comprehension.

Generally speaking, reports read well if they are written in a simple, straightforward style. There follow three examples of this, from very different reports.

We are convinced in any case that the content of many graduate training courses should be re-examined, and the inclusion of some introduction to sociological studies and the possibilities of work in practical subjects be considered. Graduates who are likely to be teaching in secondary modern schools ought to do some part of their teaching practice in those schools; and we believe that the training colleges with their experience of work in this field could have a valuable part to play in the training of these graduates.

Minimal functional testing can be performed using the marching 1's and 0's test. The memory is initially loaded with 0's in all cells. The 0 is read from the first cell and a 1 is written in its place. Read-0-write-1 replacement is continued on all other cells in order until the memory is full of 1's; then, starting at the last cell, the 1 is read and a 0 is written. This replacement is repeated until the first location is reached, decrementing the address each time. Then the entire sequence is repeated with the data reversed.

In general there are at least three factors which, by comparison with commercial operations, lessen any risk of home gardeners coming to harm when using pesticides. Firstly, as noted in the previous paragraph, the formulations available to home gardeners are usually less concentrated than those marketed for agricultural and forestry use and the application techniques are more simple. Secondly, home gardeners will seldom if ever be using a product throughout a working day. And thirdly, the fact that they may be less experienced in using pesticides may itself tend to protect them because there should then be less risk of familiarity breeding contempt and therefore a better prospect that label instructions would be read and observed.

These are infinitely preferable to the paragraph previously quoted from the pensions document.

Summary

The importance of style in report writing is the contribution it makes to readability and the effect it has on communicating the contents of the report.

The sentence is the smallest part of the structure of a report and it should be carefully considered, as the order of the words can affect emphasis and meaning. Very short sentences strung together make jerky reading, and very long ones are confusing. A sentence should not need to be read twice in order for its meaning to be extracted.

The paragraph, made up of related sentences, is a unit of thought.

When a new unit of thought is to be written a new paragraph should be started. Two or more units should not be strung together to make a paragraph of some length, but a very long unit can be divided if the sense permits.

Report writers tend to avoid using 'I' and 'we' and to use the passive instead of the active voice. This is called pseudo-objectivity and is better avoided. Equally, the excessive use of personal pronouns should be avoided.

Ordinary words should be chosen instead of out-of-the-ordinary ones, and words that add nothing to the meaning should be left out.

A simple, straightforward style is the most satisfactory for report writing.

8 Organizing Your Material and Making a Start

There comes a time when you must start writing your report. Before you put anything on paper you must be sure that you are ready. Below there is a check-list, which you should consider very carefully. If you answer 'no' to any of the questions, you are not ready to write.

1. Are you sure that you are able to provide the answer to the question that is the purpose of the report?

In the chapter entitled 'The Structure of a Report' I have pointed out that all reports answer a question. Throughout your investigation you should have borne your mandate constantly in mind, or you will have wasted a great deal of time and energy.

Each of the reports that I have used as examples has addressed a central question.

The imaginary report on absenteeism
Is there anything that the company can do in order to reduce absenteeism in its London, Birmingham and Manchester locations?

The Flixborough report
What can be learnt from this disaster to prevent an explosion from occurring at any similar chemical plant?

The Warnock report
What steps should the government take to regularize the alleviation of infertility?

The herbicide report
Is there any danger to humans and other animals if a particular herbicide is used?

2. Are you sure that your conclusions are correct?

If you have any doubt at all, your reply must be 'no', and you must reconsider your evidence. Unless you are dealing with classified material you should have tried out these conclusions on someone who is qualified to give an opinion. This is not the same thing as finding out whether your whole report is comprehensible to those who will read it.

If you are one of a committee, you must be sure that all the other members of that committee have either agreed with every point that you will present in the report or have expressed their disagreement. If there are expressions of dissent, you must take note of them and include them in the report.

3. Have you collected enough evidence to convince your reader that your conclusions are correct?

This is particularly important if readers of your report are likely to be critical of, or even antagonistic towards, your findings.

In the course of your investigation you should not have confused *quantity* with either *quality* or *relevance* of evidence. If you have conducted experiments, have you checked and double-checked your results? Have you honestly considered all the evidence, even those facts that upset any a priori assumptions you may have made or that were out of line with the rest of the evidence?

4. Have you decided to include all your evidence in your report, or are you selecting only that which seems to be necessary and relevant?

It is extremely unlikely that everything you have discovered in the course of your inquiry will be needed, but it may be so. This is not the time to decide *where* you will put this information in your report: that comes later. You need to decide at this point *what* you will include. Insufficient evidence will fail to convince your readers; too much will confuse them.

It is very important to make this selection carefully, never forgetting those who will eventually read the report.

5. Have you decided how much additional information you will include?

You do not need to weary your readers with unnecessary details; offer only the information that is necessary to convince them of the validity of your evidence and, therefore, of your conclusions. It does not matter how many times you went to London, Birmingham and Manchester to collect evidence for the report on absenteeism unless you want to parade your energy or justify your expense account. If you have interviewed someone, you must decide whether it is relevant to state that she is Miss Annabel Jones, aged twenty-nine, that she is a member of the typing pool or that she is the managing director's private secretary and has been with the company for eight years. These facts may be important, depending on the subject of the report. However, if you include that three experiments went wrong it will only show your incompetence and add nothing to the value of the report.

If you are confident about all these matters, then you will have selected all the material that you are going to use in your writing and should put on one side all the information that you have gathered and subsequently rejected. It is unwise to throw this away until the final version of the report is written, as you may have made your selection too drastically and may need to include additional information or another piece of evidence.

Your notes should be filed under the appropriate headings, and any graphs, diagrams or other illustrations should be prepared, if only in rough.

You then have to make the most important decision of all: how you are going to structure the report. The two most important factors that will influence this decision are the amount of material to be included, and who is going to read what you have written. Having made your decision it is advisable to write out the details as a skeleton around which you will build the 'meat' of your report.

At this stage you have selected the material that you will use and have decided on the framework of your report. What you are about to produce will almost certainly be a first draft. It is a mistake to think of this as only a trial run. It should be as good as you can make it. There is a sound reason for this: it is very difficult to rewrite and improve something that you have already written. It is far more sensible to think carefully about each word, each sentence and each paragraph when you first write it than to write carelessly and think that it doesn't matter because it can be corrected later.

You have to decide where you will start. It might seem that the correct way to proceed is to start at what will be the beginning of the report and to work through to the end. Unfortunately this is seldom the case, particularly for the inexperienced report writer. What might appear to be an illogical place to start, but is often the best, is at the end – your conclusions. A very important part of the process of writing is to get started, so it is often a good thing to begin by writing something that you feel confident and therefore happy about – putting into words something that can be part of your finished report.

As long as your structure is clearly in front of you, it doesn't matter in what order you produce the component parts. 'Clearly in front of you' means literally that. Having determined the structure and written it down, you will avoid repeating yourself and getting things in the wrong order if you keep strictly to it. Don't forget that you should now be thinking only about the best way of saying things, not about what you have to say. That should already have been determined. The actual labour of writing a report should not be confused with thinking out what is to be in it. Badly written reports are produced by authors who are still thinking the subject through while writing. The result of this process is inevitably confusion, particularly when the writer upsets the logic of an argument by putting things in the wrong order and by repeating information, which is not only indicative of a wrong order but is also irritating to the readers.

Most readers of a report will read through all the parts of it that they need and will then want to refer to certain selected parts again. It is part of the job of the report writer to make it easy for them to do this. One way is to give each section a heading that explains the structure of the report.

In the Warnock report the sections are called chapters; there are thirteen of these, each with a main heading. The chapters are divided into subsections, again each with a heading, and the subsections are divided into paragraphs. The first chapter is an example:

Main chapter (section)	**The General Approach**
Subsection	Background to the Inquiry (two paragraphs)
	Scope of the Inquiry (three paragraphs)
	Methods of working (two paragraphs)
	The international dimensions (one paragraph)
	The role of the Inquiry (two paragraphs)

The paragraphs are numbered; this should be done in the final draft, as it is not known in advance how many paragraphs there will be in the finished report (See pp. 102–104).

So by devising a structure, and giving headings to the main parts of that structure, you are doing two things at the same time: making it easy for yourself, in that you know what you have to include under each heading, and making it easy for the readers to find their way about the report when it is eventually finished.

To take another example, the Flixborough report is divided into main sections with headings, which are divided into paragraphs; in some cases the paragraphs are grouped under subheadings. The report begins:

heading	**Introduction** (five paragraphs)
heading	**Scope of the investigation** (four paragraphs)
heading	**Site and general history of Flixborough Works** (five paragraphs)
heading	**Layout of the works** (four paragraphs)

heading	**Organization of the Company** (one paragraph)
subheading	The Board of Directors (one paragraph)
subheading	Essential Management (five paragraphs)
subheading	The Engineering Department (two paragraphs)

The Newsom report, or *Half Our Future*, is divided into three main parts, each with a heading: 'Findings,' 'The Teaching Situation', and 'What the Survey Shows'. These are followed by acknowledgements and five appendices. Each main section is divided into chapters, each with a heading, and the chapters are divided into paragraphs. At the end of each chapter is the subheading 'Recommendations'.

Part One: Findings
    Chapter 1 Education for All
    Chapter 2 The Pupils, the Schools, the Problems
    Chapter 3 Education in the Slums
    Chapter 4 Objectives
    (and so on to Chapter 12)

Part Two: The Teaching Situation
    (Chapters 13 to 20)

Part Three: What the Survey Shows
    (Chapters 21 to 25)

Acknowledgements
Appendices

Summary

Before beginning to write a report everything must be ready. You should be able to answer 'yes' to all these questions:

1. Are you sure that you can answer the main question of the inquiry?
2. Are you sure that your conclusions are correct?

3. Have you collected enough evidence to convince your readers?
4. Have you decided how much of your evidence you will include in your report?
5. Have you decided how much additional material you will include?

Then you must decide how you are going to structure the report. This structure should be written out as the skeleton of the report. The order in which the sections are drafted is not important. It is essential to get started; therefore you should choose a section about which you feel confident. Your thinking should have been done, and your only concern now is to present the information clearly. Badly written reports are the result of thinking the problem out while writing.

Correct structuring at all levels makes writing easy and at the same time enables the readers of the report to find their way about it. The main sections and subsections of the structure should be given headings.

9 Typing and Emending a First Draft

Undoubtedly what you write to begin with will be a first draft of your report. You can write it by hand, or you can type it either on a typewriter or on a word processor. If you use a word processor, what you have put on to the disk must be printed out.

Not many report writers are more than two-finger typists, so the usual procedure is to produce a typescript of the first draft. There are three ways in which a first draft can be produced from the author's notes so that it can be read, criticized and altered if and where necessary.

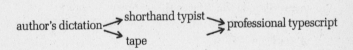

author's manuscript ⟶ professional typescript

author's typescript ⟶ professional typescript

author's dictation ⟶ shorthand typist ⟶ professional typescript
⟶ tape

Figure 42

Properly trained typists can decipher most handwriting, particularly if they are familiar with it, but they are not mind-readers. However good they are at deciphering writer's hieroglyphics, this skill is useful only if the sense of the writing is obvious. It is courteous to write reasonably legibly. Anything unusual – foreign words, medical terms, Latin tags and legal terms – should be written in block capitals. Make sure that the typist knows that the words are not to be typed in capitals. Numbers, mathematical signs or any Greek letters must be particularly carefully written.

It is not unusual for manuscripts to look like Figure 43. A competent typist, particularly one with medical experience, could have

All blood cells develop from primitive chicken cells. In adults these cells from which the red blood cells are found are found only in the red marrow of flat bones and the ends of long bones.
(the formation of erythrocytes or red blood cells.)
The stages in erythropoesy are shown opposite
The rate of erythropoesis is controlled by a glucoprotein produced in the host kidneys. It regulates the speed of mitons of reticulam cells into procryptoblants.
Factors essential to normal erythropoesis include:
* – iron (2 mg/day needed).*
* – vitamins B12.*
* – folic acid*
* – vitamin C*
* – copper.*
* – thyroid hormone corheisteroids.*

Figure 43

a good shot at typing this, but mistakes would probably occur. This
is a particularly inspired attempt:

> All blood cells develop from primitive chicken cells. In adults
> these cells from which the red blood cells or erythrocytes are
> formed are found only in the red marrow of the bone and the ends
> of long bones.

> The stages in erythropoesis (the formation of erythoates or red
> blood cells) are shown opposite.

> The rate of erythropoiesis is controlled by a glucoprotein
> produced in the . . . and kidneys. It regulates the speed of mitons
> of reliculam cells into proerythroblants.
> Factors essential for normal erythropoiesis include
>   –iron (2mg/day needed)
>   –vitamin B_{12}
>   –folic acid
>   –vitamin C
>   –copper
>   –thyroid hormone corheisteroids.

A manuscript from which the typist has a better chance of producing what the writer intended is shown in Figure 44.

All blood cells develop from primitive RETICULUM cells. In adults
these cells from which the red blood cells/are formed are found only
(or ERYTHROCITES)
in the red marrow of the flat bones and the ends of long bones.
The stages in ERYTHROPOIESIS/are shown opposite
(the formation of erythrocites or red blood cells)
The rate of erythropoiesis is controlled by a GLUCOPROTEIN—
ERYTHROPOIETON – produced in the liver and kidneys. It
regulates the speed of MITOSIS of reticulum cells into

PROERYTHROBLASTS

factors necessary for normal erythropoiesis include

— iron (2mg/day needed)

— vitamin B_{12}

— folic acid

— vitamin C

— thyroid hormone, CORTICOSTEROIDS.

Figure 44

In both examples the typist must decide whether to put in some punctuation of leave it out. Punctuation is important. Here is what a typist might produce from this piece of the manuscript:

> All blood cells develop from primitive RETICULUM cells. In
> adults these cells from which the red blood cells or
> ERYHTROCITES are formed are found only in the red marrow of
> the flat bones and the ends of long bones.
> The stages in ERYTHROPOIESIS (the formation of erythrocites or
> red blood cells) are shown opposite.
> The rate of erythropoiesis is controlled by a GLUCOPROTEIN –
> ERYTHROPOIETON – produced in the liver and kidneys. It
> regulates the speed of MITOSIS of reticulum cells into
> PROERYTHROBLASTS.
> Factors necessary for normal erythroposiesis include
> –iron (2mg/day needed)

        –vitamin B_{12}
        –folic acid
        –vitamin C
        –thyroid hormon, CORTICOSTEROIDS

Unfortunately this is not what the writer intended. The unusual words should not be typed in capital letters, and there should be spaces between certain lines. It is the writer's responsibility to make such details clear.

There are conventional ways of indicating on a manuscript how you want it to be typed. There are also terms with which you must be familiar when you are instructing the typist:

        lower case refers to small letters.
        UPPER CASE refers to capital letters

The simplest typewriter will have one typeface and you can use upper and lower case letters. So, if you want degrees of emphasis – for example, main heading and subheading – you can use:

        S P A C E D   U P P E R   C A S E   main heading
        UPPER CASE   subheading

It is also possible to underline to distinguish another heading:

        <u>Upper and Lower Case Underlined</u>   sub-subheading

More variation may be achieved by centring headings, or by aligning them with the margin, or by indenting or overhanging paragraphs. Thus a report could begin:

        M A I N   H E A D I N G
        SUB-HEADING

<u>Sub-subheading</u>

If there are to be separate sections within a sub-subheading, these may be shown either by figures or letters. Headings can also be typed in *italic* or **bold** on more sophisticated typewriters.

The writer must specify how much space is to be left between the lines of text.

Single spacing is like this:

> In the past there was considerable public ignorance of the cause and extent of infertility, as well as ignorance of possible remedies. At one time, if a couple were childless, there was very little they could do about it.

Double spacing is like this:

> In the past there was considerable public ignorance of the cause and
>
> extent of infertility, as well as ignorance of possible remedies. At
>
> one time, if a couple were childless, there was very little they could
>
> do about it.

One-and-a-half-line spacing is like this:

> In the past there was considerable public ignorance of the cause and
> extent of infertility, as well as ignorance of possible remedies. At
> one time, if a couple were childless, there was very little they could
> do about it.

The instructions that you would give to your typist in order to type out Figure 44 are shown in Figure 45. The handwritten instructions to use double-line spacing and to leave 1½-inch margins are self-explanatory. The usual method of indicating that a word should be typed differently from the manuscript is to put a line through the word and write the correct version above it, for example, the alteration of 'rate' to 'speed'. To indicate a new paragraph, double oblique lines (//) are written at the appropriate place. An arrow shows where a space is to be left. The list of elements in Figure 45 is marked to show that the lines should begin at the margin rather than being indented as they are in the manuscript. A line is drawn through the top half of any upper case letter that is to be typed in lower case.

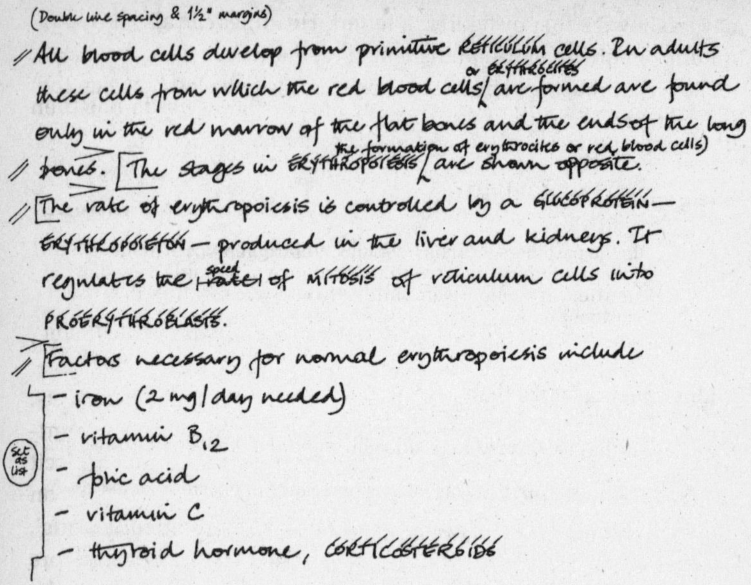

(Double line spacing & 1½" margins)

// All blood cells develop from primitive reticulum cells. In adults
these cells from which the red blood cells /are formed are found
~~or erythrocites~~
only in the red marrow of the flat bones and the ends of the long
// bones. [The stages in erythropoiesis /are shown ~~opposite~~.
the formation of erythrocites or red blood cells)

// [The rate of erythropoiesis is controlled by a ~~glucoprotein~~ —
~~erythropoieton~~ — produced in the liver and kidneys. It
regulates the ~~rate~~ *speed* of mitosis of reticulum cells into
proerythroblasts.

> Factors necessary for normal erythropoiesis include
    — iron (2 mg/day needed)
    — vitamin B₁₂
    — folic acid
    — vitamin C
    — thyroid hormone, corticosteroids

Figure 45

From the manuscript marked in this way the typist can produce
this:

> All blood cells develop from primitive reticulum cells. In adults
> these cells from which the red blood cells or erythrocites are
> formed are found only in the red marrow of the flat bones and the
> ends of long bones.
>
> The stages in erythropoiesis (the formation of erythrocites or red
> blood cells) are shown opposite.
>
> The rate of erythropoiesis is controlled by a glucoprotein —
> erythropoieton — produced in the liver and kidneys. It regulates
> the speed of mitosis of reticulum cells into proerythroblasts.
>
> Factors necessary for normal erythropoiesis include
>   — iron (2mg/day needed)
>   — vitamin B₁₂
>   — folic acid

– vitamin C
–thyroid hormone, corticosteroids.

Sometimes an author crosses out one or more words but then decides that they should be left in, for example:

The author underlines the words to be kept in and writes 'stet', which means 'let it stand', in the margin.

In a manuscript many things, such as subscripts and superscripts, are self-evident. However, if a first draft is dictated either to a shorthand typist or on to a tape, great care must be taken to give explicit instructions to the typist. For example, £23.00 should be dictated on tape as 'pounds twenty-three', and not as 'twenty-three pounds', because a fast typist will already have typed the numbers before hearing the word 'pounds'. This is a comparatively simple example, but if a complex equation has to be typed, it is probably better to write it out and indicate in the dictation where it is to be inserted. For example, it is easier to write this line of an equation:

$$1 + {}^5C_1 + {}^5C_2 = 1 + 5 + 10$$

than to dictate:

> one space plus space superscript five on the line C subscript one space on the line plus space superscript five on the line C subscript two space on the line equals space one space plus space five space plus space ten.

When dictating, unusual words must be spelt slowly and distinctly and capital initial letters specified. All words must be pronounced clearly to avoid confusion, as words such as 'affect' and 'effect' can sound alike.

If the dictation is being taken down in shorthand, or if the typist is using a word processor, additions and amendments can be put in. With taped dictation, however, insertions cannot be made unless either the typist listens to the whole tape before beginning to transcribe or the document is retyped, both of which are extremely time-consuming.

Whether a first draft is handwritten or typed by the author of the report, it is essential that there is space between the lines for alterations and additions and that there are wide margins for instructions to the typist (if it is a manuscript) and for comments both by the author and by anyone else who reads it at this stage. Only one side of the paper must be used. Adequate space must be left for diagrams, graphs and other illustrations.

Summary

There are three common ways in which the first draft of a report comes into being: it can be handwritten or typed by the author, or dictated then typed by a professional. A trained typist can usually decipher handwriting, but it is important to write legibly, taking care over unusual words, mathematical formulae, punctuation and anything that could make the typing difficult.

There are conventional ways of showing in a manuscript how the author intends it to be typed. The author should be familiar with what can be done using an ordinary typewriter with one typeface and, if the typist has a sophisticated machine, what additional capabilities this has. The typewriter can be used to show the structure of the report; main headings, subheadings, sub-subheadings and so on can be distinguished by the use of upper and lower cases, underlining and italic and bold type.

If a report is dictated, great care must be taken over unusual words. Mathematical formulae are better written, and the places where they should be inserted must be indicated in the dictation.

It is essential in the first draft, and in the finished typescript of this draft, that there are wide spaces between the lines and wide margins and that only one side of the paper is used. This allows the author to make annotations and alterations.

10 The Final Draft

So far the procedure in getting the first draft produced has been something like Figure 46. If the author or the person detailed to write the report is a competent typist, then, obviously, one stage can be left out.

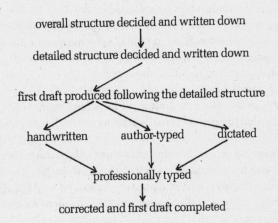

overall structure decided and written down

↓

detailed structure decided and written down

first draft produced following the detailed structure

handwritten   author-typed   dictated

professionally typed

↓

corrected and first draft completed

Figure 46

The first question to be answered is whether the first draft is acceptable as the final one. The better the preparation for writing has been, the more likely it is that little revision will be necessary. To decide this you must go back to the brief, and to the check-list that was used to prepare the first draft.

A report is commissioned to provide, if possible, an answer or some answers to a question or questions. Does the draft do this adequately? Has enough evidence been found and included in the draft to satisfy the most sceptical of potential readers? Is there anything that the readership might not be able to understand? Have you used the correct language, grammar, syntax and punctuation? You will be the first person to criticize or evaluate the draft, as you will correct and, no doubt, alter the first typescript. The next step to finding out how effective the report is, providing that it does not include classified information, is to try out the first draft on a representative sample of people.

Photocopies of the first draft, which will have been typed with double spacing, wide margins and on only one side of the paper, will provide plenty of room for readers to write their comments. One thing has to be remembered: if asked to criticize, a lot of people strain every muscle to do so. To send the photocopy back with 'OK' written at the end is thought to indicate that they haven't given sufficient attention to the draft. Therefore, an author must not be discouraged if the copies come back covered with annotations. These must be given careful consideration, and although a number of them can be easily dismissed, anything that is a genuine criticism, query, alteration or addition must be taken into account.

If a report has been produced by a committee or group of people working together, the first draft must be agreed by all concerned to make sure that the person actually writing the draft is expressing the views of all who will be held responsible for the findings. If there are slight disagreements, expressions of dissent can be recorded (see p. 85).

When you have received comments from all the people who read the first draft the next task is to prepare the second, and hopefully the final, draft. If the alterations required are considerable and important, then you must go right back to the beginning to find out where you got lost. It is usually only when the draft of a report has been written hurriedly, without adequate preparation and without due regard for the structure, that drastic revision is necessary.

Unfortunately the same procedure must be gone through again when the second draft is completed, and again, if necessary, until an acceptable draft is produced.

What happens next very much depends on the nature and purpose of the report and who is to receive it. In some cases a well-laid-out typescript, adequately photocopied, is all that is needed. This would no doubt be true of the report on absenteeism cited earlier, which would have a fairly small internal distribution.

A photocopier has become an essential piece of office equipment. If you don't have access to one, you can pay for copies to be made by a bureau. Unfortunately few copiers are kept in good condition. A photocopy should be indistinguishable from the original from which it is made, unless there is some colour involved (for example, a brown logo on the company's writing paper, which will look the same colour as the black typing on the copy). Poor copies are not only difficult to read but also give a bad impression and can nullify the value of careful layout.

Even if the report is photocopied from a typescript, it should be well presented. To put together pages somewhat unevenly and staple them together across the top left-hand corner does not make an attractive document. Plastic covers with a window are easy to come by and cheap. The first page of the report should be typed so that the title shows through the window.

Reports that will be distributed outside a company are usually typeset. This does not mean that they are printed but that they are typed on a sophisticated machine, which can produce a much greater variety of sizes, weights and styles of typeface than a typewriter or word processor. Reports that have been typeset can be photocopied on a good machine and, if the job is well done, are almost indistinguishable from those that have been printed.

The layout of a report should reflect the report's structure. If a typescript is to be copied for internal distribution, and only an ordinary machine with one typeface is available, then in order to clearly distinguish each section maximum use must be made of the different headings and arrangements suggested in Chapter 9. Below is an example of how this can be done.

REDUCING CLERICAL STAFF TURNOVER

Terms of Reference

At the board meeting of 10 July 1985, the Personnel Director was asked to instruct the Office Manager to investigate reasons for the clerical staff turnover being twice as high as that of the rest of the employees, and to recommend action to combat this.

Clerical staff turnover investigation

Summary

Records of all clerical staff appointed and leaving in the last five years were examined:
    application forms
    interview notes
    letters of appointment
    performance assessments
    letters of resignation.
	Staff records examined

The stated reasons for leaving were analysed and these were found to fall into four main categories.	Reasons for leaving established

If the report is to be typeset, either by a typist using an office machine or by a printer, conventional instructions for the layout have to be given. Before this can be done, a system of numbering for pages and/or paragraphs has to be devised.

The most important reason for numbering is to make it easy for readers to find their way around, particularly when the report is being reread and when it is being discussed. The simplest and most obvious way is to number the pages and to provide a table of contents and an index. This extract is from the table of contents in the Warnock report.

TABLE OF CONTENTS

Foreword

One ingenious and unusual system of reference is found in the index of Vernon Booth's *Communicating in Science: Writing and Speaking*. The author cites the page number, followed by a, b or c. 21a means in the top third of page 21, 31b means in the middle third of page 31, and 55c means in the bottom third of page 55.

In government reports the paragraphs are often numbered consecutively even though the report is divided into chapters. For example in the Newsom report, *Half Our Future*, we find that Chapter 7 starts with paragraph 157. This is a very easy way of finding a particular place even if the page number is not given. The numbers can become large (686 in *Half Our Future*), but there are similarly large numbers in most hymn books, yet it is not difficult to find the place.

Another way is to number separately the paragraphs in each chapter. For example, in the Warnock report the paragraphs have two numbers: the first is that of the chapter, the second is that of the paragraph. In Chapter 4 the paragraphs are numbered from 4.1 to 4.28. The index refers to paragraph numbers and not to pages – for example, 'Abortion, 1.3, 9.2, 9.6, 9.8' – which is clear if perhaps a little cumbersome.

This system can be taken further if paragraphs are subdivided:

3.2 – chapter 3 paragraph 2
3.3 – chapter 3 paragraph 3
3.3.1 – chapter 3 paragraph 3 section 1
3.3.2 – chapter 3 paragraph 3 section 2
3.3.3 and so on

Numbering can get more and more complicated, for example:

3.3.1.a
3.3.1.b
3.3.1.c i
3.3.1.c ii
3.3.1.c iii 1
3.3.1.c iii 2

But as the purpose of numbering is partly to show the structure and partly to help the reader to locate certain points of the report, it is better to make it as simple as possible.

If the report is to be typeset or printed, there are many possibilities for displaying structure and creating emphasis in the layout. As well as different sizes and faces of type, bold and italic type can be used. The typescript must be marked up so that the typesetter or printer can easily see exactly what is required (see Figure 47), which would look like Figure 48 when typeset.

(12 pt)
REDUCING CLERICAL STAFF TURNOVER

(Uc 10pt) Terms of Reference

At the Board meeting of July 10 1985, the
Personnel Director was asked to instruct the
Office Manager to investigate reasons for the
clerical staff turnover being twice as high as
that of the rest of the employees, and to
recommend action to combat this.

Clerical staff
turnover   (6pt)
investigation

(Uc 10 pt) Summary

Records of all clerical staff appointed and
leaving in the last five years were examined:
    application forms
    interview notes
LlJ   letters of appointment
    performance assessments
    letters of resignation

Staff records
examined   (6 pt)

The stated reasons for leaving were analysed
and these were found to fall into four main
categories.

Reasons for
leaving   (6pt)
established

Figure 47

One way of making reference easy, which can be seen in the above
example, is to have a wide margin on the outside edge of the page
and to print small but clear paragraph headings in that margin.

Unless the report is being printed for sale to a wide public, as
government reports are, it is advisable to leave enough space for the
readers to write their notes and comments without spoiling the look
of the pages. Some printed reports for internal circulation have one
side of each page left blank, which is useful for this purpose.

When the report is typeset a proof is supplied by the printer; then
comes the difficult job of correcting it. Authors should never proof-
read their own work, as they know what to expect and they often
read each word as they remember it and not as they see it. A misprint
is particularly likely to be missed if the word spelled incorrectly has
the same appearance as the correct word: 'rceived' will be read as
'received', 'subjcet' as 'subject'. It is claimed that almost every book
that is published contains a few errors, in spite of having been
carefully checked by several people. Psychologists call this inability

REDUCING CLERICAL STAFF TURNOVER

TERMS OF REFERENCE

At the board meeting of 10 July 1985, the Personnel Director was asked to instruct the Office Manager to investigate reasons for the clerical staff turnover being twice as high as that of the rest of the employees, and to recommend action to combat this.

Clerical staff
turnover
investigation

SUMMARY

Records of all clerical staff appointed and leaving in the last five years were examined:

Staff records
examined

application forms
interview notes
letters of appointment
performance assessments
letters of resignation

The stated reasons for leaving were analysed and these were found to fall into four main categories.

Reasons for
leaving
established

Figure 48

to see printing mistakes the 'proof-reader's illusion', although professional proof-readers are the people least likely to suffer from it. It is particularly important that figures and mathematical formulae and signs are checked by someone who knows what they are about. A good proof-reader will spot the omission in 'rceived' and the transposition in 'subjcet' but may not know that 1 365 293 should be 1 635 293, and this difference of 270 000 could matter very much indeed.

When the report is printed, it must be bound. Most large companies have their own covers, usually printed with name and/or logo, and their own machine for binding the cover to the pages. One essential is that whatever binding is used the report must open to lie completely flat. It is very irritating to read – and even more irritating to try to annotate – a book that will not stay open.

Summary

Sometimes the first draft, with a few corrections and alterations, will be accepted as the definitive version of the report. This is unfortunately rarely so. Good preparation and keeping the writing close to the agreed structure will make sure that drastic alteration will not be necessary. If it is, then the writer must go back to the original brief and consider whether the questions it poses have been answered.

To check for readability the report should be tried out on a representative sample of people. Their criticisms must be given proper consideration. If the report is of the findings of a group of people, each one must approve the draft. Then a second draft must be prepared and the process repeated until one that is acceptable has been produced.

Sometimes a well-laid-out typescript is all that is required, which, when properly photocopied and given a cover, is ready to be distributed. Good photocopies should be indistinguishable from the original.

Reports for wider distribution are usually typeset, and conventional instructions for layout must be given. A system of numbering is usually devised to make reference easy. Variations in type and layout can also help the reader by distinguishing between different sections and emphasizing certain points.

Proof-reading is difficult and should never be done by authors, who see what they expect to see. Particular care should be taken when checking numbers and mathematical formulae as a proofreader may not be able to correct mistakes in these.

For a list of standard proof-correction marks, refer to British Standards leaflet no. 5261.

11 Special Reports

Proposals

In a sense, all reports are 'selling' or persuasive documents, but some are actually offering goods or services or both for a particular sum of money. There are two sides to such a transaction, and the people on both sides need to know exactly where they stand: sellers must make it quite clear what they are giving in exchange for a stipulated amount of money, and buyers need to know exactly what they are receiving and how much they have to pay.

A report on how much will have to be paid for work and materials is called an **estimate**, though the buyer usually expects the seller to keep to this price unless it is explicitly stated that costs may vary. Often a time limit is set, so that if there is a long delay before the estimate is accepted, allowance can be made for the inevitable increase in the costs of material and labour. An estimate should also specify when the work can be done or the goods are to be received.

The most difficult reports to write are usually called **proposals**, which are particularly related to services. A proposal is an outline of work to be done, written by the **proposer**, the person or company that is to provide the service, and submitted to the **prospect**, the person or company requiring the work. Those needing others' services often invite them to submit a proposal. Consultants of all kinds – management, engineering, financial and taxation consultants – come into the category of proposal writers. Government departments ask for proposals, as do private companies.

A proposal is essentially an exercise in communication, particularly an exercise in written communication. Effective communication requires that each side should get to know the other. The proposers must endeavour to find out as much relevant information as possible about the prospect and, reciprocally, must convey to the prospect as much information about their company as will help their proposal to be accepted.

It is essential that the importance of proposals is recognized by companies selling their services. There is a time-honoured practice of giving someone who has to write a proposal or any other report a copy of the last one produced or the 'standard proposal'; the writer duly copies the shape and style, perpetuating its faults as well as its virtues. Each proposal should be a unique response to particular circumstances. The structure of a proposal for one situation may be entirely inappropriate for another.

The procedure by which a proposal comes to be written is usually as follows. An invitation to propose may come from the prospect, and this, in most cases, is followed by a meeting. The proposer must select the most suitable person or team for this meeting. The proposer then carries out investigations and submits a proposal. This will usually go through the stages outlined in chapters 8, 9 and 10. The proposal is sent to the prospect and another meeting follows, at which it is discussed. The proposal is then accepted or rejected.

As I have stressed in a previous chapter, the importance of the starting point cannot be overestimated. It is essential to know precisely what you are being asked to do. A letter of invitation to propose should make this quite clear, but if it does not, then this must be found out in discussion.

It might be that one person is briefed, writes the proposal and will carry out the work if that proposal is accepted. Alternatively one person may receive the briefing and write the proposal and select someone else to do the work. Another possibility is that one person receives the briefing, another writes the proposal and a third (or more than one person) carries out the work (see Figure 49).

A is briefed	A is briefed	A is briefed
writes the proposal	writes the proposal	B writes the proposal
will carry out the work	B will carry out the work	C or C + will carry out the work

Figure 49

It is clear that for each additional person involved there is a greater need for precise communication and a greater possibility of error, particularly when one realizes that Figure 49 shows only the proposer's side of the dialogue. There is also the prospect's side to consider – and the interaction between the two sides.

Sometimes the briefing is done by more than one and received by more than one person. As an example, the Managing and Finance Directors and the Company Secretary of a particular company may meet to brief a team selected by a firm of auditors who are proposing to be employed by that company. The Managing Director may be an engineer, the Company Secretary a lawyer, and it may be that only the Finance Director is a qualified accountant. The accountancy firm may select someone from each of their audit, taxation and management divisions. Each person will have five people with whom to communicate, which will add up to thirty communication links because each link is two-way. It is clear that if each side chooses its three people with care, and the more the proposer's side can find out about the prospect's side, the better the communication will be. It is also obvious that two of the people involved, the Managing Director and Company Secretary, might be out of their depth during much of the discussion. It should be the concern of the proposer's side to make sure that this does not happen. In this situation it is essential for there to be as much compatibility as possible between the members of each side.

Having discovered exactly what is required, the proposal must be prepared. Sometimes it is very difficult to write a proposal without doing almost as much work as would be needed to do the job.

The essential element of a proposal – whether it is for an instruction manual, written by one person, for a small company producing a computer game or for a huge undertaking (one of the foremost accountancy firms might make a bid to become auditor for a multinational company) – is that it should communicate fitness for the job. This is not as easy as it seems. If a well-established company is invited to propose, its excellence is already recognized and does not need to be stressed in its proposal, but if a small and relatively unknown company has put itself forward, then its capabilities need to be spelled out. In the first of these cases the emphasis must be on the prospect's needs; in the second, equal emphasis must be placed on the capabilities of the proposer and his understanding of the prospect's needs.

It is usually the custom to include in a proposal some information about the person or people who will be working on the assignment if the proposal is accepted. Some large companies keep standard biographies of their employees, complete with photographs. Photographs should be very recent, and a selection of professional rather than biographical data should be made to fit each particular proposal. Writing these notes should be considered part of the proposal, as the relevance of the information is what matters. Irrelevant information calculated to impress usually has the opposite effect. The knowledge that has been acquired of the prospect will help to define what is relevant.

One important difference between a proposal and other reports is that a proposal has a price attached to it. It must be made absolutely clear what will be done for that price. If, for example, journeys are to be made, the proposal must state how many and to where and whether expenses are included in the price or will be charged separately. 'Visits to three of the company's locations' could mean journeys from London to Reading, Harlow and Swindon, all quickly accomplished, or to Edinburgh, Rotterdam and Belfast, which not only take a great deal longer but are also very much more expensive. It is essential to be specific.

Once prospects become clients they sometimes like to change their mandates. This possibility must be catered for in the proposal. A few extra journeys or a change in requirements can quickly erode the profit that should be made. If the clients ask for something to be done that is not stated in the accepted proposal they must be told, before the change is made, how much extra it will cost.

Everything that has been said about writing reports in general applies to writing proposals. They must be well structured, well written, well presented and as brief as is compatible with the inclusion of all that is necessary; reference to particular sections must be easy. They must be comprehensible to all who have to read them. A good proposal may not land a job, but a bad one can certainly lose one.

Curriculum vitae

A professional worker often has to write a report on himself or herself: a curriculum vitae, or CV. This means, literally, 'the course of one's life', and is an outline of a person's educational and professional history, usually prepared for job applications. A CV, like a proposal and all other reports, is a selling document.

There is a common but misguided practice of writing down everything relating to one's education and working life, from primary school to the present day, and sending this out, suitably updated but not altered, with any application for a job or any other purpose for which it is required.

As with all reports, relevance and brevity are essential. That a candidate for a post as a communications consultant won a poetry prize at Oxford will probably not only cut no ice but may also prejudice a selection committee against him. (He might write his proposals in blank verse.) On the other hand, that the subject of a candidate's PhD thesis was some aspect of biochemistry would be interesting if the application were for a post in a pharmaceutical company's laboratory. 'Publications: *The Architecture of Oast Houses in Kent*' is unlikely to be of interest to an employer looking for a sales manager, whereas 'Publications: *The Art and Craft of Selling*' might improve the author's chance of an interview if the rest of the CV is satisfactory.

Relevance and brevity are both products of selection, and successful selection requires thought and discipline. To throw every item of information on to the paper is to imply that readers must sort them out for themselves, which, to say the least, is impolite. It also makes the assumption that the readers have plenty of time to spare. To write a CV that will be of use involves projecting oneself into the position of the reader, which, as we have seen, is an important part of every communication.

Summary

All reports are documents designed to sell something, particularly in the case of estimates and proposals. Both parties to the transaction must understand and agree on the terms and conditions contained in the report.

Proposals, which are mostly concerned with selling services, are exercises in communication. Each side must get to know the other. A good proposal places emphasis on the needs of the prospect rather than the excellence of the proposer.

It is essential to know exactly what a proposal is for, and there must be no uncertainty when the proposal is written. The more people who are involved in a proposal, the greater the chance of error; communication must be accurate and adequate between the people concerned. All that has been said about writing other reports applies to proposals. Structure and brevity are very important.

It is usual to include profiles of the people who will be involved if a proposal is accepted. These must be written specifically for each proposal and must be relevant and up to date.

Proposals have prices attached to them. Deviations from the work agreed must be paid for.

A professional worker sometimes needs to write a curriculum vitae. The writer must consider the needs of the reader and the specific requirements of the position being applied for when deciding which details to include on a CV. A CV should be brief but thorough and relevant.

12 A Check-list for Report Writers

Some people have a greater aptitude for writing reports than others. Whether their reports are good or bad is another matter; this depends on the quality of the research and investigation that precedes the writing, and this in turn will depend on the structure devised by the writer before research begins. This check-list for report writers should help to ensure that no badly written report is ever produced.

The answer to each of the questions in section 1 should be 'Yes'.

1. Have I answered the question(s) that the report posed?

   Has the investigation been carried out honestly and disinterestedly?

   Have I planned the structure of the report logically?

   In planning the structure, have I taken into account who will read the report?

   Have I put in enough evidence, but not too much, to support my conclusions?

   Have I obeyed the rules of grammar and syntax?

The answer to each of the questions in section 2 should be 'No'.

2. Have I used long words when short ones would do?

   Have I written any long and involved sentences?

   Have I used jargon unnecessarily?

   If I have needed to use jargon, have I neglected to explain the terms used for those readers who are unfamiliar with them?

   Have I repeated myself?

Are there any ambiguities?

Could this report have been shorter?

If the correct answers to the questions in each section have been given, the report should be well written.

Training and practice usually produce an improvement in any skill. Report writing is no exception to this rule.

Above all, remember:

Structure
Relevance
Clarity
Brevity

FOR THE BEST IN PAPERBACKS, LOOK FOR THE 🐧

In every corner of the world, on every subject under the sun, Penguin represents quality and variety – the very best in publishing today.

For complete information about books available from Penguin – including Pelicans, Puffins, Peregrines and Penguin Classics – and how to order them, write to us at the appropriate address below. Please note that for copyright reasons the selection of books varies from country to country.

In the United Kingdom: For a complete list of books available from Penguin in the U.K., please write to *Dept E.P., Penguin Books Ltd, Harmondsworth, Middlesex, UB7 0DA*

In the United States: For a complete list of books available from Penguin in the U.S., please write to *Dept BA, Penguin, 299 Murray Hill Parkway, East Rutherford, New Jersey 07073*

In Canada: For a complete list of books available from Penguin in Canada, please write to *Penguin Books Canada Ltd, 2801 John Street, Markham, Ontario L3R 1B4*

In Australia: For a complete list of books available from Penguin in Australia, please write to the *Marketing Department, Penguin Books Australia Ltd, P.O. Box 257, Ringwood, Victoria 3134*

In New Zealand: For a complete list of books available from Penguin in New Zealand, please write to the *Marketing Department, Penguin Books (NZ) Ltd, Private Bag, Takapuna, Auckland 9*

In India: For a complete list of books available from Penguin, please write to *Penguin Overseas Ltd, 706 Eros Apartments, 56 Nehru Place, New Delhi, 110019*

In Holland: For a complete list of books available from Penguin in Holland, please write to *Penguin Books Nederland B.V., Postbus 195, NL–1380AD Weesp, Netherlands*

In Germany: For a complete list of books available from Penguin, please write to *Penguin Books Ltd, Friedrichstrasse 10 – 12, D–6000 Frankfurt Main 1, Federal Republic of Germany*

In Spain: For a complete list of books available from Penguin in Spain, please write to *Longman Penguin España, Calle San Nicolas 15, E–28013 Madrid, Spain*

FOR THE BEST IN PAPERBACKS, LOOK FOR THE 🐧

A CHOICE OF PENGUINS AND PELICANS

A Question of Economics   Peter Donaldson

Twenty key issues – the City, trade unions, 'free market forces' and many others – are presented clearly and fully in this major book based on a television series.

The Economist Economics   Rupert Pennant-Rea and Clive Crook

Based on a series of 'briefs' published in the *Economist* in 1984, this important new book makes the key issues of contemporary economic thinking accessible to the general reader.

The Tyranny of the Status Quo   Milton and Rose Friedman

Despite the rhetoric, big government has actually *grown* under Reagan and Thatcher. The Friedmans consider why this is – and what we can do now to change it.

Business Wargames   Barrie G. James

Successful companies use military strategy to win. Barrie James shows how – and draws some vital lessons for today's manager.

Atlas of Management Thinking   Edward de Bono

This fascinating book provides a vital repertoire of non-verbal images – to help activate the right side of any manager's brain.

The Winning Streak   Walter Goldsmith and David Clutterbuck

A brilliant analysis of what Britain's best-run and successful companies have in common – a must for all managers.

FOR THE BEST IN PAPERBACKS, LOOK FOR THE 🐧

A CHOICE OF PENGUINS AND PELICANS

Lateral Thinking for Management   Edward de Bono

Creativity and lateral thinking can work together for managers in developing new products or ideas; Edward de Bono shows how.

Understanding Organizations   Charles B. Handy

Of practical as well as theoretical interest, this book shows how general concepts can help solve specific organizational problems.

The Art of Japanese Management   Richard Tanner Pascale and Anthony G. Athos   With an Introduction by Sir Peter Parker

Japanese industrial success owes much to Japanese management techniques, which we in the West neglect at our peril. The lessons are set out in this important book.

My Years with General Motors   Alfred P. Sloan   With an Introduction by John Egan

A business classic by the man who took General Motors to the top – and kept them there for decades.

Introducing Management   Ken Elliott and Peter Lawrence (eds.)

An important and comprehensive collection of texts on modern management which draw some provocative conclusions.

English Culture and the Decline of the Industrial Spirit   Martin J. Wiener

A major analysis of why the 'world's first industrial nation has never been comfortable with industrialism'. 'Very persuasive' – Anthony Sampson in the *Observer*

FOR THE BEST IN PAPERBACKS, LOOK FOR THE ⓟ

A CHOICE OF PENGUINS AND PELICANS

Dinosaur and Co   Tom Lloyd

A lively and optimistic survey of a new breed of businessmen who are breaking away from huge companies to form dynamic enterprises in microelectronics, biotechnology and other developing areas.

The Money Machine: How the City Works   Philip Coggan

How are the big deals made? Which are the institutions that *really* matter? What causes the pound to rise or interest rates to fall? This book provides clear and concise answers to these and many other money-related questions.

Parkinson's Law   C. Northcote Parkinson

'Work expands so as to fill the time available for its completion': that law underlies this 'extraordinarily funny and witty book' (Stephen Potter in the *Sunday Times*) which also makes some painfully serious points for those in business or the Civil Service.

Debt and Danger   Harold Lever and Christopher Huhne

The international debt crisis was brought about by Western bankers in search of quick profit and is now one of our most pressing problems. This book looks at the background and shows what we must do to avoid disaster.

Lloyd's Bank Tax Guide 1987/8

Cut through the complexities! Work the system in *your* favour! Don't pay a penny more than you have to! Written for anyone who has to deal with personal tax, this up-to-date and concise new handbook includes all the important changes in this year's budget.

The Spirit of Enterprise   George Gilder

A lucidly written and excitingly argued defence of capitalism and the role of the entrepreneur within it.

FOR THE BEST IN PAPERBACKS, LOOK FOR THE 🐧

PENGUIN SELF-STARTERS

Self-Starters is a new series designed to help you develop skills and proficiency in the subject of your choice. Each book has been written by an expert and is suitable for school-leavers, students, those considering changing their career in mid-stream and all those who study at home.

Titles published or in preparation:

Accounting	Noel Trimming
Advertising	Michael Pollard
Basic Statistics	Peter Gwilliam
A Career in Banking	Sheila Black, John Brennan
Clear English	Chris Magness
French	Anne Stevens
German	Anna Nyburg
Good Business Communciation	Doris Wheatley
Marketing	Marsaili Cameron, Angela Rushton, David Carson
Nursing	David White
Personnel Management	J. D. Preston
Public Relations	Sheila Black, John Brennan
Public Speaking	Vivian Summers
Retailing	David Couch
Secretarial Skills	Gale Cornish, Charlotte Coudrille, Joan Lipkin-Edwardes
Starting a Business on a Shoestring	Michel Syrett, Chris Dunn
Understanding Data	Peter Sprent